Polly Teale

Polly Teale is the Joint Artistic Director of Shared Experience.
Polly adapted and directed *Jane Eyre* and has directed *The
Clearing*, *A Doll's House*, *The House of Bernarda Alba*,
Desire Under the Elms and co-directed *War and Peace* and
Mill on the Floss with Nancy Meckler for the company.

Her other theatre credits include *Angels and Saints* for Soho
Theatre; *The Glass Menagerie* at the Lyceum, Edinburgh;
Miss Julie at the Young Vic; *Babies* and *Uganda* at the Royal
Court; *A Taste of Honey* for English Touring Theatre; *Somewhere*
at the Royal National Theatre; *Waiting at the Water's Edge*
at the Bush Theatre; *What Is Seized* at the Drill Hall; *Ladies
in the Lift* at Soho Poly; *Flying*, *Manpower* and *Other Voices*
at the Royal National Theatre Studio.

Polly's writing credits include *Afters* for BBC Screen Two and
Fallen for the Traverse Edinburgh and the Drill Hall.

AFTER MRS ROCHESTER

a play by
Polly Teale

based on the life of Jean Rhys

NICK HERN BOOKS
London
www.nickhernbooks.co.uk

A Nick Hern Book

After Mrs Rochester first published in Great Britain in 2003 as an original paperback by Nick Hern Books Limited, 14 Larden Road, London W3 7ST

After Mrs Rochester copyright © 2003 by Polly Teale

Polly Teale has asserted her right to be identified as the author of this work

Front cover photo copyright © Mark Pennington

Typeset by Country Setting, Kingsdown, Kent CT14 8ES
Printed and bound in Great Britain by Bookmarque, Croydon, Surrey

A CIP catalogue record for this book is available from the British Library

ISBN 1 85459 745 0

After Mrs Rochester was first performed by Shared Experience Theatre Company at the the Royal Theatre, Northampton on 6 March 2003 and subsequently at the New Wolsey Theatre; Oxford Playhouse; Stages at Thoresby Park; Lyric Hammersmith, London; and Guildford's Yvonne Arnaud Theatre. The cast, in alphabetical order, was as follows:

LANCELOT	David Annen
BERTHA	Sarah Ball
TITE / META	Syan Blake
MOTHER / STELLA	Hattie Ladbury
DAUGHTER / JANE EYRE	Amy Marston
ELLA	Madeleine Potter
JEAN	Diana Quick
GENTLEMAN	Simon Thorp

All other parts are played by members of the company

Writer and Director   Polly Teale
Designer   Angela Davies
Movement Director   Leah Hausman
Composer   Howard Davidson
Lighting   Chris Davey
Dramaturgy   Nancy Meckler

Many thanks to Ellen Moerman for her permission to quote from Jean's writing. Thanks also to Carole Angier for her wonderful biography of Jean Rhys which was published by Penguin Books (permission given by Rogers, Coleridge and White Ltd).

Interview with Polly Teale

as printed in the programme for the Shared Experience
production, 2003

What made you decide to write a play about Jean Rhys?

I read Jean's novel *Wide Sargasso Sea* whilst doing research
for my own adaptation of *Jane Eyre*. I was immediately moved
by the intensity of the writing, the profound sense of loneliness,
of dislocation. The introduction to the novel contained a few
details of Jean's life and it intrigued me. As I began to read the
rest of her novels, and find out more about her, a picture began
to emerge of an extraordinary life. I was struck by the parallels
between her own story and that of Mr Rochester's mad wife –
the woman who would become the heroine of Jean's late
masterpiece, *Wide Sargasso Sea*. Like Jean, Mrs Rochester
was a white Creole born in the West Indies who ended her life
isolated in the remote English countryside.

*Tell us more about Mrs Rochester – why was Jean drawn to
write about her?*

Jean first read *Jane Eyre* as a young woman. I have often
thought how startling it must have been to discover a West
Indian character hidden amongst the pages of English literature,
which made up her father's library. It is not surprising that this
creature took hold of Jean's imagination. She too was rebellious.
She too felt misunderstood. She too was prone to fits of violent
temper. Years later Jean would be sent to Holloway Prison for
biting a neighbour who she said had made too much noise and
disturbed her writing. Mrs Rochester used a similar method of
attack on unwanted intruders into her attic.

By the time we meet Mrs Rochester in *Jane Eyre*, she has
become a monster, scarcely recognisable as human. It is not

surprising that Jean felt a desire to rewrite Mrs Rochester's story, to tell it from the beginning. To tell it from the inside.

Why the locked room? Where did that idea come from?

As I found out more about Jean's life I was struck by the number of relationships she had had (including three marriages and many affairs) but how rarely she had ever felt close to anyone. She wrote, 'I've always felt best when I was alone. Felt most real. People have always been shadows to me . . . I have never known other people.'

Her own daughter never lived with Jean. She found it hard to get to know her mother. Her visits often ended in acrimony. The metaphor of the locked room began to take hold. Whilst Mrs Rochester was literally locked up and held captive, Jean was also a prisoner; a prisoner of her own psyche, of the conditions that had created her unhappy life, the schizophrenia of growing up as a poor colonial, her critical controlling mother who convinced her she was unlovable.

Jean's mother seems to be a key figure . . .

I wanted Jean's mother to represent that whole system. The fear that underlay so much of the way colonials behaved – their obsession with control and order in the face of the unknown. Although she behaves monstrously, I see her as a tragic figure born into a regime that was based on repression.

So it was Jean's mother that instilled these fears into Jean?

It must have been very confusing for Jean, she saw – and longed for – the freedom of the islanders, yet her head was crammed full of Western notions of respectability and superiority.

Do you think this schism partly explains Jean's unhappiness?

In Carole Angier's excellent biography she describes how the novelist Rosamund Lehman met Jean in later life, having admired her novels. They met for tea in a smart London restaurant. She was expecting to meet a bohemian, a kindred spirit, but Jean was a picture of poise and elegance. She was charming but distant and refused to talk about her work at all. Later, when Rosamund was invited to Jean's home, she met a different woman. Jean's husband answered the door. His face was scratched. Jean was drunk and dishevelled, muttering angrily; only half aware of her guest, whose visit she had forgotten. Rosamund stayed only a few minutes.

The need to conceal the parts of herself that she knew to be unacceptable was a constant theme in Jean's life. Her obsession with her appearance and her clothes was in part due to this. Yet in spite, or perhaps because of, her need to hide, she spoke the truth in her novels. They are as vivid an account as you will find of the dark underside of human experience, the voice of the underdog, the outsider. She speaks for anyone who has ever felt alone or afraid.

For Jean writing was not a choice but a necessity. Through it she tried to exorcise her demons. She once said, 'When you've written it down it doesn't hurt any more.'

She was not always successful. She also wrote, 'If I could put it into words it might go. Sometimes you can put it into words and get rid of it. But there aren't any words for this fear. The words haven't been invented.' (*The Sound of River*).

And yet Jean did find the words. With extraordinary honesty she strips away the layers of social behaviour and shows ourselves at our most naked, our most alone.

Jean Rhys: a Chronology

1889   (Nov) Older baby sister dies (before Jean's birth).

1890   (August) Born in Dominica – Ella Gwendolen Rees Williams.

1896   Sister, Brenda, born.

1904   (May) Goes to board at convent.

1904   Meets Mr Howard.

1905/06   Leaves convent.

1907   Sent to England.

1907/08   The Perse School, Cambridge.

1909   (Jan-July) RADA. Leaves – becomes a Chorus Girl, touring the UK.

1910   Meets Lancelot Gray Smith.

1912   Affair with Lancelot ends, although he supports her financially until 1919.

1913   Late abortion, paid for by Lancelot.

1914   Works as artists' model and 'escort'.

1917   Meets and starts affair with John Lenglet.

1919   Moves to Holland with John.

1919   (April) Marries John. They move to Paris.

1920/21   Moves to Vienna, then Budapest.

1922   Maryvonne born. Jean puts her in a Paris clinic.

1923/24   Works as shop receptionist, tour guide, artists' model, mannequin.

1924   John arrested in Paris. Sentenced to eight months in prison. Jean moves in with Ford Madox Ford and Stella Bowen. Affair with Ford Madox Ford starts. First writing published in *Transatlantic Review*. Name changed from Ella Lenglet to Jean Rhys.

1926   Affair with Ford Madox Ford ends.

1927   Jean's mother dies in London.

1928   Jean returns to England. Moves in with Leslie Tilden Smith, her agent. Sells her first novel – *Postures* (later published as *Quartet*).

1929   *After Leaving Mr Mackenzie* published.

1933   Divorced from John.

1934   Marries Leslie Tilden Smith. They are very poor and move at least three times that summer. *Voyage in the Dark* published.

1935   Jean and Leslie arrested after drunken brawl in street. Spends night in police cells and is fined for being 'drunk and disorderly' the following morning.

1938   Throws Leslie's typewriter out of the window during row.

1938/39   Writes *Le Revenant* (an early version of *Wide Sargasso Sea*) at this time, but burns the manuscript after a row with Leslie.

1939   *Good Morning Midnight* published to 'sparse and grudging reviews'.

1940   Fined for being 'drunk and disorderly'.

1945   Meets Max Hamer, Leslie's cousin.

1946   Max Hamer living with Jean.

1947   Marries Max.

1948   (March) Jean throws brick through neighbours' window.

1949   (April) Row and fight with Bezant (their neighbour). Appears in Bromley Magistrates' Court. Fined £4. Bound over to keep the peace.

1949   (May) Fails to appear for third charge of assault.

1949   (June) Charged with assault and beating Bezant. Remanded to Holloway Prison for five days for medical and psychiatric reports.

1949   (July) Sentenced to two years' probation and medical and psychiatric treatment.

1950   Max arrested. Sentenced to two years in Maidstone Prison.

1950/51   Jean disappears.

1957   *Good Morning Midnight* is broadcast, Jean is tracked down. She is working on *Wide Sargasso Sea*. Francis Wyndham, editor of André Deutsch, contacts her.

1964   Jean is persuaded to publish the first part of *Wide Sargasso Sea* in *Arts and Literature.*

1966   Max dies. *Wide Sargasso Sea* published. The novel wins the Royal Society of Literature Award and the W.H. Smith Award. Jean is made a Fellow of the Royal Society of Literature.

1968   *Tigers Are Better-Looking* published.

1976   *Sleep It Off Lady* published.

1978   Made a CBE.

1979   Jean dies on May 14. Her unfinished autobiography *Smile Please* appears.

Note

The play takes place in a room in the remote Devon country-side. As Jane begins to remember her past the characters enter her space.

Bertha Mason, Mr Rochester's first wife, remains in the room throughout the play. She is dressed in Victorian undergarments much stained and worn. Her hair is matted and dirty. She is white but speaks with a West Indian accent.

In the early parts of the play she is sleeping, with occasional murmurings and mutterings. Later, as Jean's own madness emerges she becomes a stronger presence.

In Bertha's reality the room of the play is the attic of *Jane Eyre*, where she is held captive. She is remembering her life, reliving events and talking to (arguing with) Rochester. Although she relates physically and emotionally to Jean/Ella, she is always remembering events from her own life.

The cramped conditions of the attic have given her movements an animal, feral quality. She spends much of her time on all fours.

AFTER MRS ROCHESTER

Characters

JEAN, *Jean Rhys in later life*
ELLA, *younger Jean*
DAUGHTER, *Jean's daughter*

IN THE WEST INDIES
TITE, *Ella's friend*
META, *a house servant*
MOTHER
FATHER
GENTLEMAN

FROM JANE EYRE
JANE
ROCHESTER
BERTHA, *Rochester's first wife*

ENGLAND, BOARDING SCHOOL
TEACHER
PUPIL

DRAMA SCHOOL
VOICE TEACHER

THEATRE WORLD
THEATRE MANAGER
MAUDIE, Chorus Girl
GIRL 2, Chorus Girl
GIRL 3, Chorus Girl

LANCELOT
ASSISTANT, *shop assistant*
LANDLADY
MAN, *lover*
JOHN, *Ella's first husband*

SECOND ACT
POLICE OFFICERS
FORD, *Madox Ford*
STELLA, *his wife*
HUSBAND, *Ella's second husband*

ACT ONE

1957.

A house in the remote Devon countryside late at night. JEAN RHYS's bed/ living/writing room. There is a large wardrobe containing clothes. The floor is littered with suitcases and boxes. Papers and manuscripts spill onto the floor.

BERTHA MASON, Rochester's first wife from Jane Eyre, *is lying on the ground asleep. JEAN is sitting close to her. Although JEAN is made up and dressed up there is a drunken dishevelled look about her. She has a glass of wine in her hand. She is trying to write. She speaks the following lines to herself, struggling to form the sentence.*

JEAN. Standing by the river looking at the stepping stones. The round unsteady stone. The pointed, the safe one where you stand and look around. The next one not so safe, not so safe.

We become aware of the sound of someone knocking at the front door and calling and then finally the sound of the front door opening.

With each sound BERTHA stirs in her sleep and murmurs.

JEAN checks herself in the mirror. Tidies her hair. She is agitated.

A voice, JEAN's DAUGHTER, is heard from the other side of the door. She is dripping wet.

DAUGHTER. Mother. Are you there?

The sound of the DAUGHTER trying the handle to the room. It is locked. She calls.

Mother!

JEAN. I wasn't expecting . . .

DAUGHTER. Mother, are you alright? Open the door.

JEAN. Just a moment.

> JEAN *checks herself again in the mirror. She stands nervously but doesn't walk towards the door. Meanwhile.*

DAUGHTER. Didn't you hear me outside? I've been knocking for ages. I had to find the key to the front door under the stone in the dark. I thought something must have –

JEAN. You're early.

DAUGHTER. Six o'clock. That's what I said in my telegram. I'm late.

JEAN. Saturday you said.

DAUGHTER. It is Saturday. The boat was delayed. Storms. I missed my train at Paddington. Then I couldn't get a taxi at the station.

> BERTHA *stirs. She has been disturbed by the noise. She utters something inaudible.* JEAN *looks at her panic-stricken.*

What did you say?

JEAN. I'm . . .

DAUGHTER. What?

JEAN. I'm . . .

DAUGHTER. Open the door.

> BERTHA *mutters and rolls over.*

JEAN. Busy.

> *Pause.*

DAUGHTER. What are you doing?

JEAN. I'll tell you later.

DAUGHTER. Later?

JEAN. Tomorrow. You said you were coming tomorrow.

DAUGHTER. I said I was coming on Saturday.

JEAN (*suddenly*). You turn up out of nowhere. Banging on my door in the middle of the night. Shouting. Letting yourself in uninvited.

DAUGHTER. I was invited. You said come as soon as you –

JEAN (*as* BERTHA *stirs and mutters*). Who do you think you are? Never here when you're needed. Never.

Silence.

DAUGHTER. I'm going to bed.

JEAN (*quieter*). Tomorrow.

DAUGHTER. I've been travelling for two days. I'm so tired I can hardly stand. I'll see you in the morning.

JEAN. I'm sorry.

DAUGHTER. Sorry. Yes. That's right. So am I.

BERTHA (*half audible*). Round stone not so safe, even when it dry it show slippery, even when it dry it show slippery. Slippery.

DAUGHTER. What did you say?

JEAN. Good night.

DAUGHTER. Good night.

The next day.

A tiny slither of sunlight shines into the darkened room through a crack in the closed curtains. JEAN *and* BERTHA *are asleep on the floor. There is a knock on the door.*

JEAN. Hello.

DAUGHTER. I've brought you breakfast.

JEAN. What.

DAUGHTER. Breakfast. You need to start eating properly.

JEAN. You . . . can't have. There's nothing in the fridge.

DAUGHTER. I went to the village. The woman in the shop said she hadn't seen you for weeks.

JEAN. No. I've been . . .

DAUGHTER. What?

JEAN. Busy.

DAUGHTER. Will you open the door.

JEAN. Writing.

JEAN *looks at* BERTHA *asleep.* BERTHA *rolls and murmurs.*

DAUGHTER. What's that?

BERTHA (*half audible*). Dream of escaping. In my dream I know. The passages never lead anywhere. Doors will always be shut. I know because I've been there before.

DAUGHTER. I can't hear you.

BERTHA. Passages never lead anywhere. Doors shut. Been there before.

DAUGHTER. What?

BERTHA. Been there before.

JEAN (*to* BERTHA). Be quiet.

DAUGHTER. Mother.

JEAN. Not now. Later.

DAUGHTER. What?

JEAN. I've told you I'm working. Got a deadline. The new book.

DAUGHTER. I've travelled hundreds of miles to see you. Came because you said you were desperate to see me. You said come as soon as you can. So I drop everything. Nearly kill myself to get here because I'm worried sick you're going to do something . . .

DAUGHTER *throws the tray of food to the ground.*

Open the door for Christ sake.

JEAN. I CAN'T.

Silence.

DAUGHTER. Why?

JEAN. Why?

DAUGHTER. Why ... can't ... you ... open ... the door?

JEAN. Why?

DAUGHTER. If you don't open the door I'm going to leave.

JEAN. Because ...

DAUGHTER. Did you hear me?

> JEAN*'s* MOTHER *enters the room dragging* ELLA, JEAN*'s*
> *younger self. She beats her. They both wear Victorian*
> *clothes.* ELLA *is left alone stifling her tears as* JEAN *looks*
> *on. After a while* ELLA *becomes aware of* JEAN *watching*
> *her.*

JEAN. What are you doing here?

ELLA. Go away.

JEAN. I can't.

ELLA. Leave me alone.

JEAN. I'm trying to remember ...

ELLA. Remember what?

JEAN (*gradually*). Remember ... who I was when they still
called me Ella. Remember ... why ... (*She picks up the
cane that her* MOTHER *used to beat her with.*) It's what
her parents ... What my grandparents, your grandparents
used to do to her. What they did to the slaves.

ELLA. Why?

JEAN. Because ... because they were afraid. Imagine living
thousands of miles from home on a tiny West Indian island.
Imagine twenty thousand people and only one hundred of
them white. It was terrifying.

A young black girl appears. She is dressed in a shabby colourful cotton dress much repaired and washed.

She has bare arms and legs. She swipes a book from ELLA's hands.

TITE. You want me take you somewhere you never been before?

ELLA. Where?

TITE. Yes or no?

ELLA. Give me my book back.

  TITE *withholds book making* ELLA *jump for it.*

  Yes or no?

  Silence.

  ELLA *looks at* JEAN, *who nods.*

  Yes.

  TITE *drops the book. She runs.* ELLA *follows. They use the furniture of the room like a landscape.* ELLA *watches* TITE *with delight.*

JEAN. I was not allowed to play with Tite. She could peel a mango with her teeth. Fires always lit for her. Sharp stones didn't hurt her feet. She would laugh like crazy. I never once saw her cry.

The sound of rushing water. TITE *and* ELLA *sit with their feet in the river.* TITE *is stripping a stick with a knife.*

TITE. I dare you. I dare you swim to the bottom like you say you can. Right down to the bottom. Pick up a stone and bring it back.

ELLA. I can.

TITE. I ain't never seen you.

ELLA. So.

TITE. Prove it.

ELLA. Don't have to prove anything.

TITE. You scared.

ELLA. I'm not.

TITE. Bet you can't. Bet you my pen knife. Bet you my knife and this stick and my new dress and a penny and . . .

ELLA. I bet you every penny in my purse.

ELLA *takes off her dress ready to plunge into the water as* JEAN *speaks.*

JEAN. Whenever I could escape the house I would follow Tite down to the river to swim. Past the abandoned sugar works. Into the rain forest. Where there was no road. No path. No track. Over the stepping stones. The trees grew wild there. The smell was heavy sweet and very strong. You could smell them a long way off. Huge rotting flowers drop into the water. The smell of decay, of death, and a fresh living smell.

ELLA *surfaces coughing and spluttering.* TITE *is laughing.*

ELLA. I did it.

TITE. You never.

ELLA. I did.

TITE. You look like you drown dead. You look like you drink half the river.

TITE *takes the money from* ELLA's *purse and tosses the empty purse to the ground.*

ELLA. Cheat.

TITE. Show me the stone.

ELLA. I dropped it.

TITE. Liar.

ELLA. Keep them. I can get more if I want. Cheating nigger.

ELLA *takes* TITE*'s stick.*

TITE. That not what me hear. Me hear you all poor like beggar. That old house so leaky you run with a calabash every time it rain. The garden grow wild like the forest. Won't nobody come look after it. Them say it haunted.

ELLA. Liar. You're a liar.

TITE. You eat salt fish. No money for fresh fish. You got holes in your shoes. I seen them when you take them off to swim.

ELLA. My grandfather owned Geneva plantation. He had two hundred and fifty-eight slaves.

TITE. And two hundred fifty-eight children.

ELLA. My mother had two brothers and two sisters.

TITE. That ain't what me heard. Me hear half the village your mammy's brother and sister. You look closer. See how everyone look alike round here.

ELLA *shoves* TITE *backwards. A fight begins.*

ELLA. Shut up.

TITE. Real white people got gold money. They don't come near you. They don't even look at you. You nothing but white nigger now. And black nigger better than white nigger.

TITE *climbs off* ELLA. *She takes off her dress and flings it at* ELLA. *She takes* ELLA*'s dress as well as the money and leaves.*

ELLA *gets slowly to her feet. She puts on* TITE*'s dress. She finds* TITE*'s stick lying on the ground and takes it.*

ELLA/JEAN*'s* MOTHER *grabs her by the arm and drags her into the kitchen where* META, *their servant, is drying her hands.*

ELLA. I told you. I lost it.

MOTHER (*furious*). Lost! . . . You LOST your dress. (*To* META.) Meta, find her a clean dress. Throw away that thing. Burn it.

META. Ain't no clean dress. She was wearing her clean dress.

MOTHER. Don't talk nonsense.

META. She got two dresses. Wash and wear. You want new dress drop from heaven.

MOTHER. Be quiet.

META. You want come look in the wardrobe. (*Under her breath.*) Some people crazy in truth.

MOTHER (*to* ELLA). You will go to your room and you will not leave until tomorrow when you will be clean and properly dressed. Do you understand?

Silence. ELLA *stares back at her* MOTHER, *defiant.*

Do you understand?

JEAN. That night my mother beat me so hard I couldn't breathe.

META *enters.*

Meta is rough with me in the bath saying I make trouble for her. But after, when she brushes my hair she forgets about me and sings to herself. I try not to move in case I bring her back to her senses and she tells me off again.

META *strokes* ELLA*'s hair and sings a West Indian song.*

She leaves her asleep.

ELLA *dreams of* BERTHA, *locked in her attic.* BERTHA *laughs, long and low.* ELLA *cries out in her sleep.* MOTHER *enters.*

ELLA *wakes.*

MOTHER. Shsh. You'll wake the whole house.

ELLA. I had a nightmare.

MOTHER. You made such a noise. I thought something dreadful had happened.

ELLA. It did . . .

MOTHER. I better go to your sister. You frightened her.

ELLA. I put Tite's stick under my pillow. I lie there thinking. I am safe.

JEAN *and* ELLA. I am safe.

JEAN. There is the bedroom door and the door to the house with locks and bolts. There is the garden wall and the big gates and the river and the high mountains. I am safe. I am safe.

JEAN *and* ELLA. Turn round three times, throw salt and spit.

The family gather for breakfast. ELLA's MOTHER is looking at her watch. She addresses ELLA's FATHER who is hidden from view by a newspaper. META continues to sing as she prepares breakfast in another room.

MOTHER. There is a fly in the honey and the napkins are dirty. Breakfast is supposed to be served at eight. It is half past.

FATHER. It's on its way.

MOTHER. Meta arrives late and leaves early. Every day.

Silence.

(To FATHER.) It's time you said something.

FATHER. She's just had a baby.

MOTHER. Is that my fault.

FATHER. She doesn't own a watch.

MOTHER. You never saw anyone do a thing more slowly. She's making us wait. She does it on purpose. To show us. You see the way she moves. Her head held like a queen. You ask her to hurry. She looks you right in the eye and goes even slower. No one wants to work in this country. It's a dirty word.

JEAN (*taking the fan from her* MOTHER's *hand and looking at it*). My mother always carried a fan. It was like an extra limb. Like a bird fluttering around her. Tethered. Trying to fly.

Enter ELLA.

FATHER (*to* ELLA). And how is my little tearaway? (*She sits on his knee.*)

MOTHER. She can't afford to keep the children she's got. Lord knows what she wants another one for. If *you* don't say something to her, *I* will.

Silence as META *enters with a large tray and places it on the table.* ELLA *reaches out and takes a mango from the fruit bowl. She peals it with her teeth and sucks at the juice.* MOTHER *drags* ELLA *from her* FATHERs *knee.*

MOTHER. Look at her, eating like an animal. Spit it out.

ELLA. I can't . . . I ate it.

MOTHER (*to* FATHER). You see. You see now what happens. Letting her run wild. Letting her play with whoever she likes.

(*To* META.) There will be no mangos at the breakfast table. There will be no mangos in the kitchen. There will be no mangos in the house. Do you understand.

META. What happen when them drop from the tree?

MOTHER. They rot. And if you are late again you will lose your job. (*Pause.*) You may go.

JEAN. They lay swollen and sticky. Littering the ground like tiny bloated corpses buzzing with flies. No one went near them. From that day onwards we ate hot porridge every morning for breakfast. Every morning in the sticky heat we ate porridge. It was not as strange as it sounds. Everything we owned came from England. Our clothes, our food, our newspapers.

FATHER (*looking up from his newspaper*). Grace has got another century at Gloucestershire.

JEAN. And of course, my favourite book.

ELLA *opens* Jane Eyre *and begins to read.*

*The drawing room. Thornfield Hall. During the following
sequence* BERTHA *drags herself slowly across the floor.*

ROCHESTER. Come out of the shadows Miss Eyre. I cannot
see you.

JANE reluctantly moves a little forward into the light.

Where did you come from?

JANE. A girls' school.

ROCHESTER. You were a pupil?

JANE. And then a teacher. for two years.

ROCHESTER. Your parents?

JANE. Dead sir.

ROCHESTER. Brothers and sisters?

JANE. I have none.

ROCHESTER. I thought not. Who recommended you to come
here?

JANE. I advertised, Mr Rochester. It was the only reply.

ROCHESTER. I am disposed to be gregarious tonight Miss
Eyre. Talk to me.

Pause.

JANE. What about sir?

ROCHESTER. Whatever you like. I leave the choice of subject
entirely to yourself.

Silence.

You are silent. You think me insolent. You think I have no
right to command you in such a way. I read as much in your
eye. Beware what you express with that organ Miss Eyre.
I am an expert at reading its language.

JANE looks away. He studies her.

I am old enough to be your father. I have roamed half the globe and seen much of life. Does that not allow me to be a little commanding, a little masterful once in a while?

JANE (*shyly*). You may do as you please.

ROCHESTER. That is no answer.

JANE. I don't think, sir, you have the right to command me merely because you are older than I or because you have seen more of the world. Your claim to superiority depends on the use you have made of your experience. I am, however, paid to receive your orders.

ROCHESTER. I see you are fascinated by the pattern in my carpet. My questions are a trial to you. You may leave. Tomorrow evening you will not escape so easily. Goodnight.

ELLA *and* TITE *lie on the ground.* ELLA *is reading aloud from* Jane Eyre. BERTHA *laughs.*

ELLA. I was once again in the chilly darkness of the great hall. As I climbed the stairs my thoughts were broken by an unexpected sound. It was a curious laugh. Distinct. Formal. Mirthless. I stopped. The sound ceased for an instant and then began again louder. A clamourous peal that seemed to echo in every chamber though it originated but in one.

TITE *imitates* MRS ROCHESTER*'s mad laugh. They laugh.*

TITE. What England like?

ELLA. There are ladies and gentlemen. They wear beautiful clothes and ride in carriages with velvet seats and footmen. They live in houses so big you can get lost for hours. In the winter it's freezing cold. Ice falls from the sky, but soft, like petals. It covers everything up. There's a picture on our biscuit tin. Everything white. Clean. One day I'll go to England to be a lady. I'm learning to do embroidery and play the piano.

TITE *hums a slow, rhythmic tune. This turns into the sound of the carnival passing by.* ELLA *sits embroidering. Her*

MOTHER *is fanning herself. Her* FATHER *is reading. It is very hot. A fly buzzes.*

MOTHER. Close the shutters. I've got a headache.

ELLA *gets up to close the shutters. She stands at the window, drinking in the carnival.*

ELLA. What's carnival for?

MOTHER. A lot of noise and nonsense.

FATHER. It's an ancient fertility right.

MOTHER. An excuse to get drunk and run riot for three days.

ELLA. What's fertility right?

MOTHER. I told you to close the shutters. Not stand and stare.

ELLA. It's Tite. Come and look. She's covered in feathers . . . and white paint. She's dancing. (*Shouts from the window.*) Tite . . . Tite.

MOTHER (*pulling* ELLA *away from the window*). What did I say?

FATHER. Leave her. She's doing no harm.

MOTHER. No harm. Do you want the whole town to know she was standing and staring. Watching them do those . . . those obscene . . .

As if things aren't bad enough without giving them another reason to laugh behind our backs.

FATHER. You imagine things.

MOTHER. You don't know them like I do. I grew up with them. To you it's all a novelty. They're so friendly you say. So happy. You think they're smiling at you when you walk down the street? They're sneering. Sniggering. The cranky English doctor who no one ever pays because he believes every story in the book.

ELLA (*dancing*). I want to go out. I want to dance.

MOTHER. Now look. She thinks she can do whatever she likes. And you encouraging her.

FATHER. I said it was harmless.

MOTHER. Harmless. Harmless. Do you know what they say about us?

FATHER. I don't know and I don't care.

MOTHER. The house falling down around their ears. The crazy daughter who walked down the street dressed like a nigger.

FATHER. She's a child.

MOTHER. She's thirteen years old.

FATHER. A child.

MOTHER. It's all very well for you. You're a man. You can do as you please. But a woman. A woman has to learn to fit in. To do as she's told. Who do you think will want her? Who will marry her if she doesn't know how to behave. (*To* ELLA.) Who do you think will love you?

ELLA. I don't know.

ELLA *walks stiffly back to her chair and continues to sew.* TITE *dances through the room as if in* ELLA's *imagination.*

ELLA (*as if in her head*). Who will love me? Who will marry me?

MOTHER. This heat. It's enough to drive anyone insane.

ELLA (*to* JEAN *while sewing*). Who will love me? Who will marry me?

JEAN. When you are a child you are yourself and you know and see everything. And then suddenly something happens and you stop being yourself. You become what others want you to be.

ELLA. Who will love me? Who will marry me?

JEAN *stands behind* ELLA *looking at her embroidery.*

JEAN. When it was finished it was framed. It hung on the wall at the top of the stairs. I walked past it every day. (*Trying to remember the sampler.*) It wasn't the alphabet . . . or a poem . . . or a flower. It was . . . It was . . . a . . . butterfly.

ELLA *runs towards* TITE. *She is carrying a tin in her hand.*

ELLA. It's got wings the colour of fire. Like a sunset. Like when the light shines on the sea.

TITE. Let me look.

ELLA. All the way here its wings beating on the lid.

TITE. Open it.

ELLA. I'm going to keep it. Let it out when nobody's there. Let it fly at night in the garden when . . . (*She has opened the tin.*) Oh . . . oh . . . It's broken.

TITE. You can't catch butterfly. You think you can catch sunlight. Put it in a bottle?

ELLA. I thought . . . I thought . . .

TITE. You think too much. Don't do you no good.

JEAN. I am standing by the river looking at the stepping stones. There is the round unsteady stone, the flat one in the middle, the safe one where you can stand and look around. The next one wasn't so safe. When the river was full the water flowed over it and even when it was dry it showed slippery.

Night time. The house. The sound of MOTHER *crying.*

JEAN (*to* ELLA). Where are you going? It's the middle of the night.

ELLA. I can hear a strange sound. Like an animal. Like our dog before it died.

JEAN. It is not until I am in the room that I realise. It's my mother.

ELLA*'s* MOTHER *sits on the floor. Her hair is undone and her clothes in disarray. She is folding tiny clothes and returning them to a drawer.*

ELLA. At first I think they are doll's clothes. That they are for us. For my sister and me. And then I know.

JEAN/ELLA. I know all of a sudden without doubt that there was a baby.

JEAN. A baby who died before I was born. And that baby is under the stone beneath the mango tree. And I know that I was meant to make it better . . . but I never did. And that is why our garden is haunted.

ELLA *tries to embrace her* MOTHER. *She pushes her away startled.*

MOTHER. What are you doing?

ELLA. I was . . . I wanted . . . a drink of water.

MOTHER. The kitchen.

ELLA. Yes.

MOTHER. In the kitchen.

ELLA. I'm sorry.

MOTHER *leaves.*

JEAN. I go back to bed but I can't sleep. I wish that I was dead. Perhaps if I was dead my mother would cry for me. Whenever I can't sleep I do the same thing.

She opens her copy of Jane Eyre.

Thornfield Hall. The middle of the night. JANE *throws a bucket of water over* ROCHESTER's *sleeping body. He wakes suddenly. Alarmed.*

ROCHESTER. Is that Jane Eyre? Have you plotted to drown me?

JANE. No, sir. But someone has tried to burn you alive. Your sheets were on fire. A minute later you would have . . .

ROCHESTER. Tell me quickly. What did you see?

JANE. I awoke to a strange sound. I called out but no one answered . . . until . . .

ROCHESTER. Speak out Jane. I am listening.

JANE. It was like a laugh, but low, deep, at the very keyhole of my chamber. I opened the door with a trembling hand. There was a candle dropped and burning.

BERTHA *laughs.*

ROCHESTER. You saw no one?

JANE. I heard footsteps on the stairs to the attic.

ROCHESTER. You are no talking fool Jane. Say nothing of tonight's incident. I will account for it in the morning. Now return to your room.

JANE. But who started the . . .

ROCHESTER (*sharply*). Have no fear. I can take care of myself.

Pause.

JANE. Goodnight then sir.

ROCHESTER. What, are you quitting me already.

JANE. You said I might go.

ROCHESTER. At least shake hands.

She offers her hand. He takes it in both of his. He is overcome.

I knew you would come good in some way. I saw it in your eyes when I first beheld you. Their expression did not . . . did not strike delight into my very inmost heart for nothing.

JANE. I am glad that I happened to be awake.

ROCHESTER. Will you go?

JANE. I am cold sir.

ROCHESTER. Cold, yes and standing in a puddle. Go then Jane, go.

ELLA *sits and embroiders while her* MOTHER *talks to a*
GENTLEMAN VISITOR. *They drink tea from china cups.*

MOTHER. Of course it's beautiful here . . . but impossible.
It's the heat and the humidity. We have to change our
clothes several times a day. Fabric rots. Furniture falls apart.
Nothing here lasts. Everything decays as quickly as it
grows. The road they built has almost returned to forest.
(*Offering sugar.*) Sugar?

GENTLEMAN. Thank you.

MOTHER. I grew up on the plantation but by then it was all
over. The fire had destroyed half the house. We were lucky
with the rains or they would have seen us burn with it.

GENTLEMAN. They?

MOTHER. After emancipation. Things got bad. They wanted
to see us destroyed. My grandfather had done everything he
could but it was impossible. Sugar prices were falling by the
day. England wasn't interested. Increased labour costs and
falling profits. Who in their right minds would want to
invest. And who wants a country with hurricanes and
volcanoes and who knows what up its sleeve.

JEAN. As my mother talked I watched the gentleman. He had
pale green eyes. I had never seen anyone so beautiful.

MOTHER. My husband, on the other hand, finds it all
charming and wouldn't care if the roof caved in. Which it
probably will soon if nothing is done to stop it. Excuse me.
I ordered cream tea for four o'clock.

MOTHER *leaves* ELLA *and the* GENTLEMAN *alone.*

JEAN. I knew without looking up that he was watching me.
I tried to sew gracefully but my fingers slid down the
needle. I felt sick and hot and suddenly afraid.

GENTLEMAN. So. You're the young lady who loses her
clothes.

ELLA. They were stolen.

GENTLEMAN. I see.

ELLA. But don't tell mother.

She looks at him.

GENTLEMAN. Not a word.

Silence.

Do you know you have beautiful eyes?

JEAN. That was it. That was the moment. From that day I would never be alone. I would always be watched. I must always strive to be beautiful. That was when I knew, my body was not for swimming in rivers or running through grass or climbing trees. It was my only means of survival.

ELLA *is alone in her bedroom.*

That evening I spent hours watching myself in the mirror. Hypnotised.

She imagines the GENTLEMAN *watching her.*

GENTLEMAN. Do you know you have beautiful eyes?

JEAN. It was as if I had never seen myself before.

She fantasises the GENTLEMAN *is sweeping her up in his arms and ravishing her with kisses. During the fantasy her* MOTHER *enters the bedroom.*

MOTHER. It's nearly midnight. What are you doing with the lamp still . . .

The GENTLEMAN *disappears as* ELLA *reaches for her book.*

ELLA. I was . . .

MOTHER. Yes?

ELLA. Reading.

Picks up Jane Eyre.

JANE *stands in the middle of the room wearing her wedding dress without a veil.* BERTHA, *elsewhere, holds a piece of paper to her head and then tears it to pieces.*

JANE. Standing sir, at the end of my bed in the darkness, scarcely further than you are from me now. She had thick, black hair hanging long down her back. I watched as she took my wedding veil from its box: she held it up, gazed at it long, then threw it over her head and turned to the mirror. Oh sir, I never saw a face like it. It was a discoloured face. A savage face. The lips were swelled and dark. The eyes hunted. I saw her then take the veil from her head and rent it in two parts, flinging both to the floor. Now sir, before we go to the church, tell me, who and what that woman was.

ELLA *reads aloud to* TITE. *They are lying together on the ground. Sound of the river.*

ELLA. He answered me without hesitation. 'The creature of an over-stimulated brain. I must be careful of you my treasure. Nerves like yours were not made for rough handling.' (ELLA *closes the book.*)

TITE. What happen next?

ELLA. They go to the church but in the middle of the wedding a man shouts for it to stop. It turns out Mr Rochester is married already. He's married to the woman who escapes at night from the attic. And guess where she comes from?

TITE. You've read it before.

ELLA. Five times. Guess.

TITE. I don't know.

ELLA. The West Indies. He came here and married her. (*She reads.*) I instantly fell in love with that tropical clime where the light is golden and the air warm. (*Addressing* JEAN.) How did Charlotte Brunette know?

JEAN. She made it up.

ELLA. She never came here?

JEAN. She lived on the Yorkshire moors.

ELLA (*reading*). I walked amidst the dripping mango trees of my wet garden. Amongst its drenched pomegranates and pineapples. Mosquitoes hummed . . .

JEAN. She used to read the travelogues in the back of her father's newspaper.

ELLA (*looks up from the page*). When we're grown up and married let's still come and meet at the river.

TITE. Me thought you going to England. Become a lady.

ELLA. Promise.

TITE. Live in house you get lost. Can't never get out.

ELLA. Say we will.

TITE. I ain't getting marry.

ELLA. You have to.

TITE. Say who.

ELLA. Everybody. You have to marry . . . You have to marry if you want to . . .

TITE. My mother ain't marry.

ELLA. But how did she . . . she's got children. . . You've got to be married to . . .

TITE (*laughs*). Sometimes you is like a baby. Sometimes you is too stupid to be a baby. (*She laughs and laughs.*)

ELLA *sits embroidering with her* MOTHER.

ELLA. Mother. It's true isn't it. You have to be married to have a baby?

MOTHER (*taking the embroidery*). You've pulled it too tight. Look, you've nearly made a hole.

ELLA. That's right isn't it? You have to be married to –

MOTHER. Look at that stitch. It's twice the size of the one before.

ELLA (*defiant*). So what.

MOTHER. What did you say?

ELLA. So . . . what.

MOTHER. Unpick that row and start again.

ELLA. Mother. Are we poor?

MOTHER. Who said that? Who told you that?

ELLA. Tite.

MOTHER. You are forbidden to speak to –

ELLA. She says we eat salt fish because we've no money for fresh fish.

MOTHER. That's enough.

ELLA. She says we're poor like beggar. She call us white niggers. She say half the village my brothers and sisters because grandfather he have babies with lots of black ladies.

MOTHER. Go to your room. Get out. You're disgusting.

ELLA. Liar. You're a liar. I hate you.

ELLA *suddenly picks up the embroidery and pulls the cloth from the sampler tearing it in two. She smashes the hoops to the ground.*

ELLA *runs to her room and throws herself onto the ground. She picks up* Jane Eyre.

From here onwards the two scenes run concurrently.

ROCHESTER *unlocks the door of the attic.* JANE, *dressed in her bridal gown, stands beside him.* BERTHA *hides in a corner of the room snarling.* JANE *stares in horror at the creature in front of her.*

ROCHESTER. That is my wife whom I married fifteen years ago in Spanish Town Jamaica. Bertha Mason is mad. Just how mad you will see for yourself.

MOTHER *enters* ELLA's *bedroom.*

MOTHER. Well. What do you have to say for yourself?

Silence. ELLA *continues to read in a show of defiance.*

BERTHA *scurries to and fro, snatching and growling. When she sees* ROCHESTER *she looks confused.*

BERTHA *cries out, rearing up.* BERTHA *snaps and snarls like a cornered animal.* ROCHESTER *moves towards her.* ROCHESTER *slowly stretches out his hand.* BERTHA *whimpers. Her eyes fill with tears. She nuzzles his hand. She reaches out towards him trying to kiss him.* ROCHESTER *pushes her away appalled. Suddenly* BERTHA *springs forward grappling with* ROCHESTER, *as if trying to strangle him. She lays her teeth into* ROCHESTER*'s shoulder.* ROCHESTER *struggles violently. He forces* BERTHA *to the ground.*

At the same moment MOTHER *raises her stick to beat* ELLA. ELLA *springs towards her, biting her arm and wrestling the stick from her hand. She raises it above her head ready to attack. She freezes.*

MOTHER. I've done my best. It's no use. You'll never learn to be like other people.

JEAN. There it was. I had always suspected it but now I knew.

ROCHESTER *and* JANE *disappear.* ELLA *continues to stare at* BERTHA. *She listens to her* MOTHER*'s voice.*

MOTHER. She flew at me like an animal. It was frightening. There's nothing I can do with her. I've tried but it's no use.

JEAN. Like an animal. Frightening.

ELLA *stares at the creature in front of her.*

META *packs* ELLA*'s suitcase.* ELLA *takes the suitcase.* ELLA *continues to stare at the strange shape of* BERTHA MASON.

META. There are some tamarinds in syrup, and guava jelly, and cassava cakes.

META *squeezes* ELLA *goodbye.*

MOTHER *puts out her cheek for* ELLA *to kiss goodbye.*

ELLA *still stares at* BERTHA.

JEAN. They sent me to the convent at the other side of the island. I would make myself good. I would learn to be like other people.

ELLA. I wept for Jesus and put stones in my shoes to punish myself for evil thoughts. I learned to cover my body when I washed or dressed, even if I was alone. I learned about that most precious possession. That flawless crystal that once broken could never be mended.

JEAN/ELLA. Once I prayed for a very long time to be dead.

JEAN. The convent was my refuge . . . from myself. Until . . . one afternoon I am told there is a visitor. I am excused from evening prayers.

ELLA *and the* GENTLEMAN *sit side by side in the garden. They each have a cup of tea.*

JEAN. He is disappointed. My eyes are no longer beautiful. I am ugly and awkward and he wishes he never came.

ELLA (*trying to sound like her* MOTHER). The weather is very . . . pleasant today but tomorrow they say it will rain.

GENTLEMAN (*speaks aloud*). They dress you quite hideously here.

ELLA. I hope you had a pleasant journey.

GENTLEMAN. If you belonged to me I would seldom allow you to wear clothes at all.

JEAN. He knew.

GENTLEMAN. Would you like to belong to me? You would wait on my guests naked and if you dropped anything you would be punished.

JEAN. He'd seen at once that I was not a good girl who would object, but a wicked one who would listen.

GENTLEMAN. How old are you?

ELLA. Fourteen.

GENTLEMAN. Quite old enough to have a lover.

The GENTLEMAN *puts his hand into her blouse.*

JEAN. I wrote to my mother. I told her I didn't want him to visit me.

MOTHER *enters.*

MOTHER. Your uncle is extremely kind to make the effort to come to see you. You will take care not to be rude and be clean and wear your best dress and new shoes.

JEAN. That year he came to see me at the convent often. And I waited for him to come. Counted the days.

GENTLEMAN. Love is not about happily ever after. It is about violence. Violence and humiliation. I love you.

MOTHER. How often has he been?

ELLA (*defiant*). Twenty times. Maybe more.

MOTHER. What did he talk to you about?

ELLA. He told me . . . stories.

MOTHER. What about? Were you alone?

ELLA. We sat in the garden.

MOTHER. What did you wear?

ELLA. My best dress. And new shoes. Mother, I want to tell you –

MOTHER. Your father and I have decided that you should go to school in England. It will be for the best. You can finish you education and then find yourself a husband. Your father and I can't afford to keep you after that.

Trunks and cases are loaded onto the boat. The sound of the ship's horn as it prepares to leave. ELLA *and her* FATHER *shout above the noise.*

ELLA. Where's mother?

FATHER. Headache. Can't bear the heat. Locked up in her room with the shutters drawn.

ELLA. Tell her . . . Tell her I . . .

JEAN. Tell her I . . . Tell her I . . .

ELLA *is left waving as if from the deck of the ship. Steam. Whistles. Sound of the sea. She waves and waves and waves.*

ELLA. Sargasso Sea. Why does it sound so sad. There are some words that are too sad to say . . . Like mountain . . . or . . . mother. (*To* JEAN.) Sargasso Sea. They say that there are weeds. You can't see them from above. They grow beneath the surface. Wrap themselves around. They can pull whole ships down. Or make you turn in circles and drag you back the way you came.

Sound of the ship's whistle. Cases carried on shore.

The train. Everyone hidden behind newspapers.

JEAN. England. It was as if a curtain had fallen, hiding everything I had ever known. The colours were different. The smells different. I watched it through the train window, divided into squares like pocket handkerchiefs. A small tidy look it had. Everywhere fenced off from everywhere else.

Boarding school. England.

TEACHER. This is the dormitory. You are expected to make your bed every morning. Breakfast is at six thirty. Lessons begin at eight. You are not allowed to speak except when spoken to by a teacher. You are forbidden to run or walk abreast in the school building. If you leave the building you must wear a hat and gloves. No running or shouting in the grounds. If you leave the school grounds you must have written permission.

TITE appears.

TITE. You want me take you somewhere you never been before?

As the TEACHER continues to list the school rules TITE clambers over the furniture. She is making her way down to the river.

TEACHER. If you do as you are told.

TITE. Yes or no?

TEACHER. And follow the rules I'm sure we will get along fine.

ELLA *(to TITE)*. Yes. Yes. Yes.

JEAN. Everywhere white people. Even the cleaners and the lady who mended our clothes were white. And I soon discovered that I was a curiosity. They would ask me to repeat certain words and then fall about laughing.

ELLA. My voice. My hairstyle. The way I sang. Everything about me was different. I couldn't ride a bicycle or play hop-scotch or name a matinée idol.

JEAN. School was mostly spent copying from the board. In English we were sometimes allowed to invent a story. A great deal of attention was paid to our spelling and punctuation. The content of the story was never mentioned. But that term we were studying *Jane Eyre*.

ELLA sits beside another GIRL in English class. They are reading aloud.

SCHOOLGIRL. Just give me a few moments Jane. That is all I ask. Just a few moments and you shall see how the case stands. I arrived in the West Indies, a young man full of the excitement of six weeks on the open seas. I fell instantly in love with that tropical clime where the light is golden and the air warm. Mangos grow on the trees Jane. There are flowers that open at night and blaze like fires. It was as if

I had arrived in paradise. She was an exquisite creature.
Raised to enchant. To seduce. To entice. A marriage took
place before I knew it.

BERTHA *emerges from the trunk dancing.*

SCHOOLGIRL. We were married only a few weeks before I
discovered her true nature. I found her tastes obnoxious.
Her mind low. She would get drunk and then erupt in
outbreaks of violent and unreasonable temper. She had an
appetite for every kind of excess, and yes . . . for other men.

TEACHER. Thank you Gilly. Ella.

ELLA. I lived with that woman for four years at the end of
which the doctors declared her mad. She was shut up in her
bedroom and tended by a nurse. You could hear her curses
night and day. No harlot ever had a fouler vocabulary than
she.

TEACHER. So Ella, you and Bertha Mason come from the
same corner of the globe. Perhaps that explains a few . . .
eccentricities.

The class giggle. The school bell rings.

TEACHER. For next week five hundred words on the use of
flower imagery in chapter forty two.

The class disappears.

ELLA *is left alone still holding her copy of the book. She
stares at* BERTHA, *still dancing.*

ELLA (*reads*). Whether beast or human being one could not
tell. It grovelled on all fours. It snatched and growled like
some strange wild animal . . . but it was covered with
clothing. A quantity of dark, grizzled hair hid its face.
(ELLA *looks up from the book.*) What is she doing here?

JEAN. She lives here.

ELLA. I don't want her here. I travelled five thousand miles to
get away from her . . . How did she . . .

JEAN. You brought her here.

ELLA. Tell her to go away.

JEAN. She can't.

ELLA *opens* Jane Eyre, *rips out handfuls of pages and flings the book across the room.*

ELLA. I must get away . . . As soon as I can . . . Get away. Away.

BERTHA. Must get away. Soon as can . . . Get away. Away.

JEAN. The Royal Academy of Dramatic Art. It was written above the door in beautiful curling letters.

BERTHA. Must get away. Away.

JEAN. At last, I thought. My life is about to begin.

ELLA (*writes home*). Dear all. Having a wonderful time. Yesterday we learned how to die. You fall forward if you're stabbed from behind. Backward if you're stabbed from the front and straight down if you stab yourself. We also learned how to laugh. You sing backwards very quickly down the scale.

The Royal Academy of Dramatic Art. The VOICE TEACHER *repeats a phrase to* ELLA. ELLA *tries to say it in R. P. But her voice retains its West Indian sound. The* TEACHER *is clearly exasperated.*

VOICE TEACHER. *Oh* what a *rogue* and peasant slave am I. Repeat.

ELLA. Oh what a rogue . . .

VOICE TEACHER. *Oh* what a *rogue* . . .

ELLA. Oh what a rogue . . .

VOICE TEACHER. *Ohhhhh* . . .

ELLA. Ohhhhh . . .

VOICE OF TEACHER (*exasperated*). That will be all for today.

ELLA. I'm sorry . . . I . . . can't seem to hear . . .

TEACHER. I'm afraid if your accent isn't gone by the end of term you will have to leave.

ELLA. Leave. But I only just got here.

TEACHER. It would be irresponsible of us to encourage you further.

ELLA. But . . . I'm sure I can –

TEACHER. With that voice you wouldn't get a job in the circus let alone the theatre.

ELLA. What is it? What's wrong with it?

TEACHER. Frankly. (*Beat.*) You sound like a nigger.

MOTHER *enters.*

JEAN. Your father and I were most distressed to hear about your recent dismissal. It confirms my doubts about the whole business of your going on the stage.

MOTHER. The best you can do now is find yourself a good husband. A professional. Not drinker or gambler. Try to make the most of yourself. Stand up straight and don't talk too much or laugh too loud. You have red in your hair so have to be very careful how you dress. No scarlet or pink. Stay out of the sun or your freckles come out like a rash. You profile is too pronounced so avoid being seen from the side. If you offer an opinion do so . . .

ELLA *screws up the letter.*

ELLA *stands in front of a* THEATRE MANAGER. *He looks her up and down. She sings the lullaby that* META *sang to her as child.*

MANAGER. How tall are you?

ELLA. Five foot three inches.

MANAGER. Small, but pretty enough. Age?

ELLA. Eighteen.

MANAGER. Let's see your legs.

> ELLA *lifts her skirt and turns. The* THEATRE MANAGER *chuckles.*

No need to look so miserable. You're hardly Tetrazzini but you've got yourself the job.

> *The* THEATRE MANAGER *gets a costume from the wardrobe and hands it to* ELLA. *As he talks the* CHORUS GIRLS *arrive on stage helping one another to dress.*

You're paid thirty-five shillings a week and five extra for matinées. It's a copy of the London show so watch it as many times as you can. They'll give you standing room at the back. Two weeks rehearsal. You have to pick it up quick or you're out. There are two other companies touring the country. Three nights in each town. Luggage travels ahead with the scenery.

ELLA. Yes. Thank you.

MANAGER. Don't tell the other girls you went to acting school. They might not like it.

ELLA. Thirty-five shillings a week. Twenty for lodgings. Three for food. Six for travel. One for stockings. That leaves . . .

JEAN. Thank God for matinées.

An excerpt from the show. ELLA *is in the chorus.*

The dressing room. The GIRLS *all crowded into a small space, removing clothes and makeup.*

MAUDIE. Landlady smiled at me today. Said 'Good morning'. Bet she puts it down on the bill.

GIRL 2. Good morning. Two Shillings. Good morning with a smile. Two shillings and six pence.

MAUDIE. Sunday night we arrive to the toughest joint of roast beef you ever tried to cut with a knife. Thank goodness that's over I thought. Monday it's warmed up. Tuesday it's minced. Wednesday it's become Shepherds pie. Thursday stew. Friday soup. Saturday I think surely to God it'll be something else. But no. 'I've saved a little bit for you.'.

During this speech the THEATRE MANAGER *appears at the door with a letter for* ELLA.

THEATRE MANAGER. From London. Swanky writing.

GIRL 2 (*handing* ELLA *the letter*). Decent club.

MAUDIE. Which.

GIRL 2. Brooks.

They all crowd around as ELLA *opens it.*

GIRL 3. Who's it from?

ELLA. He came backstage in Southsea. Wants to take me out tomorrow night after the show.

GIRL 2. Say you're busy.

MAUDIE. Say you're having supper with a friend.

GIRL 2. Say you're free Saturday week when we're in Holloway. Get to see Brooks. They always spend more money at the weekend.

MAUDIE. I've just bought some stockings. Cost nearly a week's wages. You put a hole in them and I'll kill you.

ELLA. Thank you.

The GIRLS *leave.* ELLA *looks through the wardrobe.*

ELLA. What am I going to wear?

JEAN. Your best frock.

ELLA. It's got a hole under the arm.

JEAN. The ball dress Aunt Clarice handed down.

ELLA. Doesn't fit. I've had it altered twice but it's worse than ever.

JEAN (*picking something out of the case*). What about this?

ELLA. The cuffs have worn through.

JEAN. Ask wardrobe for a bit of lace.

ELLA *has put on the dress. She tucks under the cuffs.* JEAN *mirrors her as she looks at herself in the glass.*

LANCELOT *appears on stage. He is dressed in expensive clothes. He is pouring champagne into a glass.*

LANCELOT. Tell the driver I'll be late. And bring some more champagne . . . and some truffles.

ELLA (*looking at herself in the mirror of* JEAN). It'll have to do.

JEAN. Well hurry along. He'll be waiting.

ELLA (*remembering advice from the* GIRLS). Always ten minutes late. Enough to make him think you might not be coming but not enough to make him give up and go.

JEAN. Good luck.

ELLA *stands in front of* LANCELOT. MOTHER *appears as if in* ELLA's *head.*

MOTHER. Profile too pronounced. Try to avoid being seen from the side. If you offer an opinion do so . . .

JEAN. Oh God. I am ugly and awkward and he wishes he never . . .

ELLA *sneezes.*

LANCELOT. Your hands are frozen. Come and have a seat by the fire.

ELLA. I was born . . . I grew up in the West Indies. I'm not used to the cold.

JEAN. Sit up straight. Make the most of yourself.

LANCELOT. Take my jacket. (*He puts it around her shoulders.*)

ELLA. Sometimes I close my eyes and try to imagine the warmth of a fire is the warmth of the sun. (*She laughs.*)

JEAN. Don't talk too much. Don't laugh too loud.

LANCELOT. What brought you to England?

ELLA. My family. It was decided . . .

ELLA *looks at her* MOTHER.

MOTHER. Your father and I have decided you are going to
school in England. You can finish your education and then
find yourself a husband. Your father and I can't afford to
keep you after that.

LANCELOT *tries to kiss her. She pushes him away
violently.* MOTHER *remains on stage.*

LANCELOT. I'm terribly sorry. Forgive me. You looked so
lovely and so sad I . . .

ELLA. Don't try to stop me or I'll make a frightful row.

ELLA *heads for the door.*

LANCELOT. Look. Listen. It's raining and you've got a
dreadful cold already.

She sneezes.

Let my man run you home. I'll send my doctor over in the
morning. Please.

He takes her hand.

Sit down.

She allows him to lead her to a chair.

Are you often ill like this in winter?

ELLA. Last winter I had pleurisy. The company had to leave
me behind in Newcastle.

LANCELOT. By yourself?

ELLA. Three weeks I was there but it seemed like forever.

LANCELOT. Poor darling.

JEAN. Say that again. Say darling again like that.

LANCELOT. Poor darling.

BERTHA *sniffs at* LANCELOT *rubbing her face into his hand. She whines with desire.*

ELLA *sneezes.*

LANCELOT (*hands her his handkerchief*). Here.

She kisses him politely and then with abandon.

JEAN. I am safe. I am safe. There is the warm fire and the smell of furniture polish and the thick carpet. There are the servants and the door man and the tall railings. I am safe. I am safe.

BERTHA *is coiled around* LANCELOT *rooting out his smell. He begins to remove* ELLA's *clothes. Suddenly he stops himself.*

LANCELOT. Can I ask you something? Is it your first time?

ELLA. No.

LANCELOT. You ought not to lie about that.

ELLA. It doesn't matter. It's not important.

LANCELOT. You have beautiful eyes. Did you know that?

He carries her to bed.

JEAN. Afterwards he put some money into my hand bag when he thought I wasn't looking.

LANCELOT. The car's waiting. (*He kisses her forehead.*) I'll write.

ELLA. The driver winks at me but I pretend not to notice. I am thinking about what clothes I'll buy. When I speak my voice sounds round and full. Instead of small and thin.

JEAN. That was because of the money.

ELLA. I'd like to go to Cohen's in Shaftesbury Avenue and then on to the milliner's in Dean Street and to Parker's on the Mall and then . . .

JEAN. I had often looked through the window of Cohen's. There was always an outfit in the window that made you feel sick with longing. And always a well-dressed woman inside surrounded by boxes and shop assistants.

ELLA *enters the shop.*

ASSISTANT. Can I help you?

JEAN. She is too quick with her request. I realise that she is looking at my clothes. She doesn't think I can afford to buy anything.

ELLA. Yes. I'd like to try the coat in the window. Is it for sale?

ASSISTANT. Of course.

The ASSISTANT *takes a coat from* JEAN's *wardrobe. It has a fur collar and a glamorous expensive look.* BERTHA *nestles her face into the folds of the fabric. She sniffs hungrily.*

ELLA. As I try on the coat I can feel my whole life changing.

ASSISTANT. Would you like to see yourself in the mirror madam?

ELLA. Changing into the life I would lead if I was the owner of the coat. In this coat I will go to all the lovely places I've ever dreamed of. In this coat no one will ever know.

She looks at BERTHA.

JEAN. How much is it?

ELLA. I don't know. There isn't a price tag.

JEAN. Then ask.

She looks at herself in the mirror. It is everything she hoped it would be.

ELLA. Yes thank you. I'll take it.

JEAN. What if you can't afford it?

ASSISTANT. Would madam be needing anything else?

JEAN. What if you haven't got enough money?

ELLA. No thank you. That will be all.

ASSISTANT. I have a very pretty little evening dress that would suit you.

ELLA. Not today.

ASSISTANT. The spring ball gowns arrive next week madam, if you'd like to call again.

ELLA. Yes. Thank you. I will.

ASSISTANT. Shall I? (*Meaning 'take it off'.*)

ELLA. No thank you. I'll keep it on. I'm a little chilly.

ELLA *leaves the shop wearing the coat. She feels like a movie star.*

ELLA. There was sixpence change from the twenty-five pounds he'd given me. I sent the taxi away and walked. Everything was different now as I'd known it would be. People made room for me in the street. Men were courteous not leering. I saw women in thin shabby coats look at me with envy. Twice someone asked me for money. I felt like a queen.

She sits down finally. The LANDLADY *enters.*

LANDLADY. I'm afraid Miss Rhys I'm going to have to ask you to relocate on Saturday. This room is reserved after Saturday.

ELLA. Why didn't you tell me when you let it to me?

LANDLADY. I don't hold with the way you go on if you want to know and my husband don't either. Staying out all night and then today dressed up to the nines. I've got eyes in my head.

Fantasy.

BERTHA *snarls at the* LANDLADY.

ELLA. Take your revolting little room you nasty, mean-lipped, uptight, two-faced . . .

Reality.

ELLA. I'll vacate by midday. Thank you.

JEAN. He found me a room with a dressing table and pretty curtains overlooking a square. He gave me money every week. It was both humiliating and exciting. I was a kept woman. It meant I belonged to him and I wanted to belong to him, completely.

MAUDIE *from the chorus stands in the middle of* ELLA*'s room. She pours them both a drink. She has a bruised eye.*

They drink. MAUDIE *checks out* ELLA*'s coat.*

MAUDIE. Swanky coat.

ELLA. Cohen's.

MAUDIE. Whatever you do don't fall in love with him. Don't get soppy. Keep your head screwed on you could do well out of this.

ELLA. What happened to your eye?

MAUDIE. When you think he's really fallen. That's the moment to get what you can. Because it won't last. Never does. Don't wait too long. That's fatal.

ELLA. Did he hit you.

MAUDIE. Get him to buy you a flat. Somewhere nice up West.

ELLA. He says he loves me.

MAUDIE. He does does he.

ELLA. I love him.

Pause.

MAUDIE. You've told him haven't you.

ELLA *runs to* LANCELOT. *She clings to him, nestling into his coat.* BERTHA *nuzzles his hand.*

ELLA. I never wanted to live before I knew you. I always thought it would be better if I died. Why did you make me want to live? Why did you do that to me?

LANCELOT. Why?

ELLA. Once, when I was a child, I used to sleep with a piece of wood by my side so that I could defend myself. That's how afraid I was.

LANCELOT. Afraid of what?

ELLA *and* JEAN. Of nothing. Of everything.

JEAN. That year the spring was beautiful. I had no idea that England could be so beautiful.

JEAN *and* BERTHA *are together as the scene unfolds.*

LANCELOT (*to the driver*). Number twelve Judd Street.

ELLA. Aren't we going to go to . . .

LANCELOT. I'm frightfully tired. Have to be up early.

ELLA. I thought we . . .

LANCELOT. If someone asks you what you do say you're an actress. Don't mention the chorus. They get the wrong idea.

ELLA. I was only telling the truth.

LANCELOT. Yes but you saw the way he looked at you. You know what people are like.

ELLA. I don't care.

LANCELOT. Well you should care. Anyway I'm going to help you get on. I'm going to arrange a singing tutor. And dance classes. You'd like that wouldn't you?

ELLA. I don't know.

LANCELOT. What do you mean you don't know. That's what you want isn't it? To be a success.

ELLA. I want to be with you.

LANCELOT. Oh you'll soon get sick of me.

JEAN. And I knew then that he wanted me to get sick of him.

BERTHA *starts to whine.*

I had become like a stone he was trying to roll up a hill that always rolls down again.

ELLA. Tell me you love me.

LANCELOT. Look there's something I need to tell you. I'm going to New York for a month or so. You'll be taken care of while I'm away. But when I come back I ... I don't think we should see one another.

Silence.

It's not that I don't love you. I do. In fact I think you're worth more than this. You should meet someone who can ...

BERTHA. Don't understand. Him not understand. Think I want more than I do. As long as I can see him sometime. Whenever. Where ever.

ELLA. Could we ... I'd like to ...

BERTHA. If I never see him again I die.

ELLA. Can we go back to your place. I need to talk to you.

BERTHA. I'm dying already.

LANCELOT. I'm sorry. I have someone staying. I need to be up early.

BERTHA/JEAN. The kind of excuse you make to a stranger. An idiot. To someone you despise.

LANCELOT. Look this is terribly difficult. You know how much I care about you but you must have known ...

ELLA. What?

LANCELOT. That it wouldn't ... It couldn't ...

BERTHA (*shouts*). Why not?

ELLA. Why not? ... No ... I didn't.

LANCELOT. I'll arrange for you to receive some money each week. And you can stay in the flat until you find something else. (*Reaches in his pocket for his purse.*) Here's something to tide you over.

She stares at the money. He puts it into her pocket.

ELLA. I'll let you know my new address.

LANCELOT. Of course.

BERTHA *howls with grief. ELLA and* BERTHA *collapse in a heap.*

JEAN. I found a room. Somewhere. Anywhere .I didn't care. I closed the curtains and got into bed. For two days I wrote letters.

ELLA (*writing*). I'd like to see you just once more. It needn't be for very long. It need only be for an hour. (*Corrects.*) Half an hour.

BERTHA *screws up letter. As she speaks* ELLA *writes half speaking the words along with her.*

BERTHA. Me love you. Me love you. Me love you. You can't do this to me. If I were a dog you wouldn't do this to me. I wish I *was* your dog so that I could follow you and smell you and sleep at the bottom of your bed and eat the scraps you throw under the table and lick your shoes and have you beat me . . .

ELLA *continues to write down* BERTHA's *words as* JEAN *speaks.*

JEAN. For three days I wrote without stopping. Page after page. I didn't sleep. Didn't eat. On the third day I caught the last post.

She reads the final letter.

ELLA. I am now living at number ten Offord St. I hope your trip is a success. Regards Ella.

JEAN. I put the rest of the pages in a chocolate box and locked them in a suitcase. When you've written it down it doesn't hurt so much. But you're finished. A part of you is gone.

BERTHA. Part of you gone. Lost . . . Washed up.

JEAN *slumps on top of* ELLA *and* BERTHA. *They lie together in a heap.*

JEAN. You'd be amazed how much you can sleep if you really put your mind to it. Fourteen. Sixteen. Eighteen hours a day. When you sleep like that you don't dream. It's as if you're dead. You want to be dead.

ELLA. One morning I woke up feeling sick. It's the same the next day.

MAUDIE *enters and pulls* ELLA *to her feet.*

MAUDIE. You can't stay there for the rest of your life.

ELLA. Why not?

MAUDIE (*offering her drink from a hip flask*). Mate of mine. He's got a friend. You'll like him. He's funny. That's what you need. A laugh.

ELLA *slow dances with a* MAN. *They kiss. He begins to undress her.*

ELLA. Why am I doing this?

JEAN. You're looking for him.

ELLA. He's in New York.

JEAN. For a part of him.

ELLA. He's in New York.

BERTHA. Sometimes the sound of his voice or the way that he walks. Or sometimes his shoulders . . . or his smell or . . . the taste of his mouth . . . his sweat . . . sweet sweat . . .

ELLA *starts to resist as he pulls up her skirt.*

ELLA. Why am I doing this?

MAN. Are you joking. I've just paid for a three-course meal and enough champagne to sink a ship.

He has sex with her. Leaves money.

MAUDIE. *Never* go back to his. Not even if he looks like the dog's bollocks. They're the worst. Hotel's best. Make sure he's paid for it mind. Always someone around if you get into trouble. (*Picks up money left by the* MAN.) You should be charging more than that.

ELLA (*shocked*). I'm not . . . I didn't . . .

MAUDIE. You can move in with me if you like. Look out for one another. It's safer that way. We'll do well.

ELLA *vomits into a jug.*

MAUDIE. You're not? . . .

ELLA *shakes her head.*

MAUDIE. Are you sure?

ELLA *shakes her head.*

ELLA. How can you tell?

MAUDIE. Jesus. You're a baby ain't you.

ELLA. Don't worry. I'm going to drink a bottle of gin and jump out of the window and that'll be the end of it.

MAUDIE (*looking out of the window*). No it won't. You're not high enough. You jump out of here you'd just make a mess of yourself. Have to live like that. All smashed up for the rest of your life.

ELLA. What shall I do?

MAUDIE. I know someone. It'll cost you more because you left it so long.

JEAN. I wrote to him in New York. He sent me a cheque and then a huge box of chocolates on the big day. When he came back he visited me. Brought me flowers. He cried and told me how much he loved me. He went back to New York the next day without a word. I received a letter in the second post.

ELLA. I have been instructed by my client to pay the sum of five pounds and two shillings to Miss Ella Gwendoline Rhys every Friday until further notice. Please acknowledge receipt and oblige.

ELLA. I'm going to send it back.

JEAN. You'll need it.

ELLA. Who does he think he is. To pension me off like some servant.

BERTHA. How dare he. Insult me. Treat me like a prostitute. A whore. Like a slave.

JEAN. Tomorrow you'll have to pay the rent.

ELLA. I'm going to tear it into a hundred pieces. Burn it. Send him the ashes.

JEAN. Or you could cash it.

BERTHA. I hate him. Loathe him. Wish I never met him.

ELLA. The next day I cashed the cheque. And every week after that.

JEAN. You can get used to anything.

ELLA. You think I'll never do that.

JEAN. Never.

ELLA. And then you find yourself doing it.

> ELLA *opens her compact and powders her face.*

JEAN. And then the war. The clubs and cafés shut down over night. The men disappeared. I found it hard to imagine the war. We read the newspapers. Everyone talked about it, but it was hard to believe that somewhere somebody was in the middle of it. My shoes leaked and I couldn't afford a new pair. I took a job in the chorus of a West End show.

JEAN. What was it called? (*Trying to remember.*)

ELLA. Our Miss Gibbs.

JEAN. One night on the tram home I sat next to a man who had been at the theatre.

> JOHN LENGLET *speaks with a Dutch accent.*

JOHN. This dancing. This dressing up. Is not good for you.

ELLA. Why not?

JOHN. I think that you waste your life pretending.

JEAN. I was absolutely furious. And absolutely captivated.
A month later when he asked me to marry him I said –

ELLA. yes.

JEAN. I was saved, rescued, fished up, half-drowned out of the deep dark river. Dry clothes. Dry hair. No one would know I had been in it. Except of course that there always remains something.

JOHN *lifts* ELLA *in the air.*

JOHN. Let us leave this country. Is no good for the soul. It make heavy. Make sad. Too much raining.

ELLA. My dear Lancelot. I am soon to be married to a brilliant Dutch journalist and writer. We are going to live abroad so I will be leaving my London address. The lawyer's cheque will no longer be necessary.

JEAN. When we stepped onto French soil I knelt down and thanked God for getting me away from England. I vowed that I would never go back. Never. Whatever happened. Whatsoever.

ELLA. Where are we going?

JEAN. To Paris and then Vienna.

ELLA. What's Vienna like?

JEAN. Beautiful. Like a mirage. Like an opera set.

BERTHA. That old house so leaky you run with a calabash every time it rain.

JEAN. Like a place in a dream you can never remember.

BERTHA. No one don't come to look after the garden no more.

JEAN. It smelt of lilac and drains and of the past.

BERTHA. That garden grow wild like the forest.

JEAN. There are parties every night. There are beautiful women in exquisite clothes. And money.

BERTHA. No money for fresh fish.

JEAN. Oh great God money.

BERTHA. You eat salt fish.

JEAN. You make possible all that is good in life. The envy of men. The love of women. Even the luxury of a soul and thoughts of one's own.

BERTHA. You got holes in your shoes.

JEAN. At last I was safe.

BERTHA. I seen them when you take them off to swim.

JEAN. There was the flight of steps to the front door. Chandeliers, mirrors, oceans of carpet. The taffeta day dress and the satin gown with the silk roses . . .

BERTHA. You ain't nothing but a white nigger.

JEAN. . . . the velvet. The organdie and . . .

ELLA (*still dancing*). And if you could have chosen.

BERTHA. And black nigger better than white nigger.

ELLA. If you had had the choice between being a writer and being happy, what would you have chosen?

JEAN. To be happy of course. To be happy.

A knocking is heard on the door of JEAN's *room. We are back in the present.* JEAN's DAUGHTER *is at the door. We hear her dimly through the music.*

DAUGHTER. Mother . . . Mother.

JEAN. Not . . . now.

DAUGHTER. I need to speak to you.

JEAN. I've got . . . a visitor.

DAUGHTER. What did you say?

JEAN. Visitor.

DAUGHTER. I'm going to leave. If you don't open the door I'm going. I'll go to the phone box. Book a taxi. Get the first train I can. Do you hear what I'm saying. I'm going to go unless you open the door.

ELLA *and* JOHN *sit. He has his hand on her stomach.*

JEAN. The first morning I was sick I thought I must have eaten
something. But the next morning was the same. After a
week I knew.

DAUGHTER. Mother.

JEAN. The doctor said 'congratulations' and I wept.

DAUGHTER. Mother, I mean it. This is your last chance. I'm
going to go unless you open the door. Is that what you
want? Is that what you want me to do? Do you hear? Do
you hear what I'm saying to you?

Interval.

ACT TWO

JEAN*'s room as before.* JEAN*'s* DAUGHTER *still standing at the door.*

DAUGHTER. I'm going mother . . . unless you open the door right now . . . Do you hear?

John is sitting beside ELLA. *He has his hand on* ELLA*'s stomach.* ELLA *is heavily pregnant.* BERTHA *is lying close by.*

JEAN. Did I want a child? . . . No.

DAUGHTER. Can you hear me?

JEAN. But lying on that sofa in that dark, cool room, I felt a sense of power.

DAUGHTER. I'm going and I'm not coming back. I mean it.

JEAN. As though I were a magnet. I was absorbed. Exalted. Lost.

BERTHA (*to herself*). No road. No path. No track. Rotting flowers. Drop into the water. Smell. Sweet and strong. The smell of death. Decay. And a fresh . . . living smell.

DAUGHTER. Right. That's it.

DAUGHTER *leaves.*

Inside the room JOHN *kisses* ELLA*'s forehead and goes.*

A MAN *enters with a* WOMAN *who begins to search the room.*

ELLA. Who let you in here? Who are you?

MAN. Where is your husband?

ELLA. Out. I don't know.

MAN. When will he be back.

ELLA. Who are you? What do you think you're doing?

MAN. Have you any idea where he's gone?

ELLA. You will leave this house immediately or I'll call the police.

MAN. We are the police.

The WOMAN *shakes her head having found nothing. They leave.*

JEAN. We left in the middle of the night with a car boot stuffed full of dresses. We drove without stopping.

ELLA. Where am I going?

JEAN. Somewhere. Anywhere. Where no one knows who we are.

ELLA. But I'm about to have a baby. (*She feels a pain from the baby.*) Where will I have the baby?

JEAN. A place for people without money. When I arrive at six o'clock in the morning they tell me there isn't a place. They tell me to come back at four in the afternoon.

ELLA. Four in the afternoon.

JEAN. It is the longest night of my life. When they try to put her into my arms I refuse.

ELLA. I don't like her. I have been too much hurt.

JEAN. She is taken to the clinic. I promise I will come and get her as soon as I have a place to live. (*Turning on* ELLA.) *you* promise.

BERTHA. Six flights of stairs. Forty-five steps. A stain on the ceiling. Getting bigger. It smells of disinfectant and another smell they're trying to hide.

JEAN. You promised.

ELLA. He goes away to look for work. If we can get money we can get a better room. I am an English tour guide. (*As if addressing a group of tourists.*) The fountain on your left was a Valentine's present from the King to the Queen. (*To* JEAN.) My breasts are dripping milk. Stains appear on my coat. I get us lost in the Parc Monceau and can't find an exit until the gates are closed for the night. I become a shop assistant but I insult a customer. I become an artist's model but I can't stop crying.

JEAN. She was your child.

ELLA. I can't stop crying.

JEAN. Your daughter.

ELLA. My husband is arrested and sentenced to eight months for fraud.

JEAN. You said you'd go and get her as soon as you . . .

ELLA. For five days I eat nothing but the slice of bread we are given for breakfast.

Silence.

I am told that somebody knows an English man, Madox Ford, who will pay people for writing.

ELLA *opens a suitcase and takes out an envelope full of scribbled pages. The 'letters' she wrote to* LANCELOT *in Act One.*

I give her a name. The girl who wrote the letters. I write another twenty pages and send it.

FORD MADOX FORD *enters taking the pages out of her hand.*

FORD. The ending is melodramatic. Too predictable. Of course in life people do commit suicide. But in art it is better to keep them alive. People will say that you didn't know how to end it.

ELLA. I didn't.

FORD. Exactly.

ELLA. Nor did she.

FORD. It feels too abrupt. Meaningless. As if you had no idea
where you were going.

ELLA. I didn't.

FORD. And there is too much self pity. Of course we all have
days when we feel like that, but it's relentless. The other
characters have no life of their own. They are seen entirely
through her eyes. You cease to have any sympathy.

ELLA *gets up and crosses the room. She takes the
manuscript and goes to exit.*

I want you to rewrite.

ELLA. Money. I need money.

FORD. I'll pay you two hundred francs. You can use your
beginning but I want her to survive. She is about to throw
herself into the river when she changes her mind.

ELLA. Why?

FORD. That is for you to decide.

ELLA. Why? Why if it's so dreadful do you want more?

FORD. It's frighteningly alive. Dark. Truthful. I have never
read anything like it.

ELLA (*imagining the next few lines of the story*). She walked
back with her hands in her pockets and her head down. Next
week or next month or next year she would kill herself. But
she might as well last out her month's rent, which had been
paid up, and her credit for breakfast in the morning. She
was soon back on the street where she lived. Opening the
front door.

ELLA *writes as she speaks and continues to write as*
BERTHA *speaks.*

BERTHA. Six flights. Four landings with ten doors. All shut.
Forty-five steps. Forty-five or forty-six. I lose count. Too
tired to count. Too tired to sleep. Too tired. And there are so
many hours left to live. So many. People say that life is
short but it's not if you don't want it. It go on and on and on
and . . . Never ending. No ending.

JEAN. The night I deliver the story it's raining.

ELLA stands dripping wet holding the manuscript.
STELLA, FORD's wife, has answered the door.

STELLA. My goodness. Let me take your coat.

ELLA. It's alright. I just came to deliver . . .

JEAN (*looking at* ELLA). Her dress was well cut. Her hair
recently styled. She was definitely of the species of wife.

FORD enters. ELLA gives him the manuscript.

ELLA. I would have put it through the letter box but it
wouldn't fit.

FORD. So. She survives.

ELLA. Just about.

FORD. You'll stay to dinner.

ELLA. I . . . have to get back.

FORD. Tell cook to set another place at table.

ELLA. Really I . . .

FORD. You can't go back this evening. You're half drowned
already.

JEAN. And so I stayed.

ELLA, FORD and STELLA are eating dinner. ELLA eats
hungrily. BERTHA sits beneath the table. ELLA feeds her
scraps when no one is looking.

STELLA. The driver wants a schedule for the weekend. I told
him I hadn't a clue but he keeps pestering. Really it is too
much trouble. I far prefer our life in the country where we
live like peasants and never spend a penny.

FORD. Stella thinks that money is the root of all evil.

STELLA. Well really. Life gets so complicated.

JEAN waits on them as if she were a servant carrying a
tray with wine and glasses.

JEAN. Have you noticed how it is always rich people who tell
you that money isn't important. Sitting in their beautiful
homes in their expensive clothes they tell you that money is
nothing but a nuisance. Of course, if you talk to anyone
who's ever wondered where the next week's rent is coming
from they'll tell you the truth. How anyone can expect a
decent human impulse, a single altruistic thought from
someone with holes in their shoes I do not know. Poverty
does not make you brave and resourceful it makes you
jealous and angry and ashamed. In a world that tells you
'Spend. Spend. Spend and you'll be happy.' To be poor is to
be nothing. And they wonder why there are thieves.

FORD (*to* ELLA). More wine?

ELLA. Yes please.

STELLA. Forgive me. I'm exhausted. Ford will show you to
your room. It's been a pleasure.

STELLA *leaves.* ELLA *stands. She is unsteady on her feet
after too much wine.*

ELLA. I'm sorry. I really have to go.

FORD. And why is that?

ELLA. My husband will be waiting.

FORD. No he won't.

ELLA. He's expecting me.

FORD. He's in prison.

Pause.

And you are going to come and live with us. You can write
in the mornings and translate in the afternoons. The great
works. From English to French. You will soon learn how
to tell a story.

ELLA. But what if I don't want to tell a story. What if I don't
think life has much of a story. Except when we dress
ourselves up and talk nonsense and pretend to be something
we're not. What if life is just one long miserable muddle.
One big mess, with no one to pick up the pieces?

FORD. If life has no story that is precisely why literature must. We are all of us adrift. All of us alone and afraid and searching for meaning. That is why we read. Why we write. Why we talk to one another. We are hoping to bridge that great chasm between ourselves and others. To find ourselves in a story.

ELLA. I don't know . . .

ELLA/JEAN. I don't know.

FORD *kisses* ELLA.

BERTHA. You are thirsty. Dried up with thirst and yet you don't know it until someone hold up water to your mouth and say 'drink'.

FORD. Do you know you have beautiful eyes?

JEAN. You stayed.

ELLA. Yes.

JEAN. But you said you'd go and get her. You promised. You told her.

ELLA. All my life before I knew you was like being lost. Lost on a cold dark night. Tell me you love me.

STELLA *enters. She is talking to a friend.* ELLA *is listening.*

STELLA. I must say I was staggeringly slow to realise they were in love. Yes of course she was pretty, but she was so lost, so self absorbed. Terrified of everything and everyone. I hadn't realised how exciting it can be for a middle-aged man to rescue a foundling. He published her first book of stories. Changed her name to something dreadful he says sounds more modern. Jean, I think it is. He tells her what to read. What to wear. Of course he's in love with her. He created her.

Pause.

I don't believe in making scenes about things. It can't last long. He'll get tired of her soon enough. She's hardly Wife material.

ELLA *pulls clothes from the wardrobe, stuffing them into her suitcase.* FORD *follows her to and fro.*

FORD. You can't leave. You've got nowhere to go.

ELLA. Get out of my way.

FORD. Wait until the morning. What will Stella think?

ELLA. She knows.

FORD. What?

ELLA. I heard her. Talking to a friend.

FORD. You've had too much to drink. You're tired and upset. Go to bed. We'll talk about it tomorrow.

ELLA. That's right. You don't believe in making scenes about things do you. It's not proper. Let's carry on as if nothing has happened until you get sick of me and throw me out. That's how it ends isn't it? That's how the story ends. Or is that too melodramatic, or meaningless, or predictable.

FORD. Alright. So you want a row. Well let's have one. Don't try to pretend you didn't want this as much as I did. After that first kiss I apologised. Promised that was the end of it. But you wanted it. Trailing around the apartment half dressed. Looking at me with those big eyes. Sobbing on my shoulder. Pressing your body against me. But I kept off you didn't I. I knew I could have you just by putting my hand out but I didn't do it. But there comes a limit. I've been watching you and I knew that someone else would get you if I didn't. You're that sort.

ELLA. How dare you.

FORD. Look. You've every right to be like that if you want to. And I've every right to take advantage of it. But don't come to me with all this sob stuff. Making out I'm the villain.

BERTHA. Sob stuff. Sex stuff. That's the way men talk. They look at you with their cold eyes. It's wrong. Everything wrong.

ELLA. Get away from me.

FORD *tries to take her in his arms but she struggles against him.*

FORD. Look. You know I'm in love with you. I've wanted you since the first time I saw you. I was burning up. Tortured.

BERTHA. No past. No future. Nothing but the taste of his mouth.

FORD. If you're not happy here we must find you a hotel. Tomorrow we'll go and find you somewhere. Somewhere nice.

BERTHA. When he hold me I think I was lost before I know him. All my life before I know him like being lost on a cold dark night.

ELLA. At first he came to visit every day. I would dress up and wait for him to arrive. Excited. Like a school girl. My heart beating.

JEAN. He always hurried the end of his dressing as if getting out of the room was an escape. He would say he had to go somewhere. Anywhere that didn't involve saying her name.

FORD *leaves.*

BERTHA. But now him gone. I wait for the sound of his feet on the stair.

JEAN. The room smells of stale scent. I imagine all the women before me who have waited here. All the hours and hours spent waiting.

ELLA *begins to write down everything that* BERTHA *says.*

BERTHA. At night the clock tick so loud I shut it away in a drawer, but I can still hear it. After a while I throw it against the wall so now there isn't any time here. All smashed up. Broken. No more tick tock. No more story. No beginning. No ending. Nothing but the words in my head. Talking. Talking. Won't stop. Throw it against the wall. Won't stop. Shut up. Shut it. Shut.

ELLA (*writing*). No more story. No beginning. No ending. Nothing but the words in my head.

JEAN. I start to write it down. Anything to get it out of my head. For a while afterwards there is quiet . . . and then it starts up again.

BERTHA. Talking. Talking. Won't stop. Throw against the wall. Won't stop. Shut up . . .

ELLA. If I could put it into words it might go. Sometimes you can put it into words and get rid of it.

JEAN. But there aren't any words for this fear. The words haven't been invented.

FORD *enters.*

FORD. No wonder you're miserable. Who wouldn't be, stuck in here all day. Why don't you go somewhere. Do something.

BERTHA *paces the room.*

ELLA (*still writing*). I go to a café but people stare at me because I'm alone. I go to the zoo but there's a fox in a cage. Up and down it ran. Up and down. Each time it turned with a certain hopefulness. As if it thought escape were possible.

JEAN. He doesn't come the next day. Or the next. Or the day after that.

ELLA. Of course I know the rules. I can't go to his house or telephone or put a note through his door.

BERTHA. I can't throw a stone through his window. Smash a bottle in his face.

ELLA. Be quiet. Shut up.

BERTHA. Be quiet. Shut up. Silence. Shut your face. Shut it. Shut up.

FORD *returns.*

FORD. It must have gone astray. I sent it to the hotel. What else could I do.

ELLA. Where were you?

FORD. Stella needed a weekend away. It hasn't been easy for her all this.

ELLA. Oh yes. That's right. Stella clicks her fingers and you do whatever she wants.

BERTHA *joins in, speaking the same words as* ELLA.

While I have to wait like a dog under your table for the scraps you sling down. Mustn't make a noise. Mustn't whimper or I might get kicked in the teeth. Mustn't bite or I might never get fed again.

BERTHA *snarls.*

FORD. That's enough.

ELLA. While she stuffs her face at the table.

FORD. You have no idea how foolish you appear to me when you insult Stella.

ELLA. Insult her. I'd like to kill her. I'd like to smash a bottle over her head and watch her . . .

FORD. I will give orders to the concierge not to let you up in future. I'm not going to have Stella threatened. Do you hear?

BERTHA. Be good to me. Be kind to me. Something broken. Something in me broken. Sorry. I'm sorry.

FORD. Do you hear what I'm saying to you.

ELLA. Sorry. I'm sorry.

BERTHA. Sorry. So sorry. Shut up. Hit me. Hurt me. Make me. Sorry. I'm sorry. I. So sad. So aching.

ELLA *starts to rip up the story she has been writing. She turns on herself, hitting her head and sobbing hysterically.* FORD *tries to stop her, holding her in his arms. They begin to undress one another.*

After sex. Him dressing.

ELLA. When will I see you?

FORD. I'll send a telegram.

ELLA. Tomorrow?

FORD. Perhaps.

ELLA. I love you. I'm sorry. I just . . . I miss you.

FORD. I'm late.

ELLA. Don't go.

FORD. Look. I'm sure you must know what I'm going to say.
It can hardly come as a surprise the way things have been
between us . . . I don't want to . . .

ELLA. I try to decide what colour I shall have my hair dyed.
Shall I have it red. Shall I have it black. That would be
startling. Shall I have it blond cendre.

JEAN. But blond cendre madam is the most difficult of colours
to achieve.

FORD (*hands her a bundle of notes*). There is some money. It
won't last forever but it will give you a chance to get
yourself on your feet.

ELLA. The thing is to have programme. No leaving things to
chance. No gaps. No trailing around with cheap
gramophone records starting up in your head.

JEAN. No 'here this happened. Here that happened.'

ELLA. Above all no crying in public.

FORD. We are going away for some time. Out of the country.

ELLA. Have a plan and stick to it. First do one thing and then
the next.

FORD. I'm sorry it has to be this way but I really don't see
any alternative.

ELLA. I will buy gloves. Buy scent. Buy lipstick. Buy
anything cheap.

JEAN. Just the sensation of spending. That's the point.

ELLA. Bracelets studded with artificial jewels. Red, green and
blue. Necklaces of imitation pearls.

FORD. Please don't come to the apartment or try to contact me.

ELLA. Cigarette cases. Jewelled tortoises. Earrings.

JEAN. You receive a letter. Your mother is dying. Please come as quickly as you can.

ELLA. I must go to her. Must go.

JEAN. It was posted six months ago. Redirected four times.

ELLA *collapses to the floor.*

ELLA. What happens now?

BERTHA. You spend days, weeks, crying. Staring at the wallpaper.

ELLA. And after that?

BERTHA. The ceiling.

ELLA. And then?

BERTHA. The wallpaper.

ELLA. Who am I? How did I get here? (*To* BERTHA.) Who are you? Where did you come from?

BERTHA. No road. No path. No track. Trees grow wild. Huge rotting flowers drop into the water. Smell. Heavy and sweet. Smell of decay and a fresh living smell.

ELLA. I need to see my daughter.

BERTHA. Fresh. Living . . .

ELLA. I'm going to go to see her. I spend two hours putting on make up. Putting on clothes. Trying to make myself look like other people.

JEAN. Trying to make myself look like someone who might be somebody's mother.

ELLA *is standing in front of a five-year-old child. The child is* JEAN*'s daughter.*

ELLA. She doesn't recognise me. The nuns have to tell her who I am. I try to think of something to say to her. (*Speaking to the child.*) What's your favourite colour?

JEAN. She doesn't know.

ELLA. Pick one. Any one. It doesn't matter.

JEAN. She still doesn't know.

Silence.

ELLA. Let's . . . make up a story. You start.

JEAN (*as* DAUGHTER). What about.

ELLA. Whatever's in your imagination.

JEAN. She can't think of anything.

ELLA. So I make up a story.

JEAN. It's about a woman locked in a room who can't remember how she got there.

ELLA. She is frightened by the story and tells me to stop. She wraps herself in a curtain and refuses to come out. I have to call one of the sisters. (*She is close to tears.*) I'm going to come back for you. I'm going to get some money and then I'm going to come back. (*To her* DAUGHTER.) You're going to come and live with your mummy.

ELLA *packs clothes into her trunk.*

ELLA. Where am I going?

JEAN. To England.

ELLA. But I told you. I'm never going back there. Not ever. Whatever.

JEAN. You do.

ELLA. What for?

JEAN. To find a literary agent.

ELLA. Do I find one?

JEAN. You marry him.

ELLA. But I'm never going back there. Not ever. Whatever.
I swore.

JEAN. You marry him.

ELLA. Has he got money.

JEAN. No. But he's kind. He loves you. He can read your
dreadful hand writing. He types up your novel. And then
the corrections. And the corrections of the corrections. And
the . . .

ELLA *is reading a hand-written page of her novel. She has
a pen in her hand to make corrections.*

ELLA. It was as if a curtain had fallen, hiding every thing
I had ever known. The colours were different. The smells
different. I watched it through the window, divided into
squares like pocket handkerchiefs. A small tidy look it had.
Everywhere fenced off from everywhere else. (*To her*
HUSBAND.) There should be a full stop after window, so
that the words are fenced in like the meaning. A full stop
instead of the comma.

HUSBAND. It's too late.

ELLA. What is?

HUSBAND. I sent it on Friday.

ELLA. Sent it! You sent it without telling me.

HUSBAND. You've been correcting it for months. You should
write something new. Let it go.

ELLA. Should. I should, should I?

HUSBAND. You need a break.

ELLA. Do you think this is something I can pick up and drop
whenever I fancy. Do you think this is something I choose
to do? Do you think I have a choice?

HUSBAND. I meant you need to –

ELLA (*enraged*). Don't tell me what I need to do. What do you know about what I need. What I don't need is someone doing things behind my back like I'm some kind of imbecile. Some kind of idiot.

HUSBAND. I thought it was for the best.

ELLA (*screams*). It wasn't ready.

She attacks him. Pummelling his chest. He takes hold of her wrists. She collapses.

They'll hate it. I know they will.

JEAN (*triumphant*). A letter arrived the next day. They want to publish.

ELLA. Does anyone buy it?

JEAN. A few brave souls.

ELLA. What do they think?

JEAN (*looking at reviews. She reads*). Impressive. Original. A remarkable book. Flawless. Subtle and tender.

ELLA (*spotting one that* JEAN *is avoiding*). What does that one say?

JEAN. A sordid little story.

BERTHA *stirs.*

ELLA. That one.

JEAN. A waste of talent . . .

ELLA. And?

JEAN. Miss Rhys proves herself to be enamoured with gloom to an incredible degree. Her heroine is a pitiful and uncomfortable human being.

ELLA (*looking at* BERTHA). That's her fault.

JEAN. Yes.

ELLA. Why is she here?

JEAN. The door's locked.

BERTHA. Four walls. A door. Room empty. Them don't leave nothing no more. No trace. No clue. There is a window too high to see out of. Where am I. How did I get here? How did . . . How did I . . .

ELLA. But why is she here . . . with me?

JEAN. You brought her here.

ELLA. Tell her to go away.

JEAN. She can't.

ELLA (*to* BERTHA). Leave me alone.

JEAN. She can't.

ELLA. This is my room. I live here.

JEAN. So does she.

BERTHA. Something broken. Stopped ticking. Stopped like a clock. Smashed up./ mash up. Everything broken. Everybody broken.

BERTHA *repeats the line underneath* ELLA.

ELLA. Tell her to shut up. Stop talking. (*To* BERTHA.) Can you hear me? Shut up. Shut it. Shut your . . .

BERTHA. Shut up. Shut the . . . Smashed up. Broken. Everything broken. Somebody help me . . . Somebody . . . Can anybody hear me?

ELLA *grabs* BERTHA, *putting her hand over her mouth and wrestling her to the ground.*

ELLA (*to* JEAN). My daughter's coming. I don't want her to know . . . She mustn't . . .

JEAN. I know.

JEAN *hands* ELLA *the red wine.* ELLA *feeds the wine to* BERTHA *like a* MOTHER *feeding a baby milk.* BERTHA *is finally subdued. She sinks down onto the floor.* ELLA *covers her up and then applies make up. She is preparing for the arrival of her* DAUGHTER. *During the next sequence* ELLA *addresses the child. She is nervous. Doing her best to be 'normal' although she has been drinking.* BERTHA *makes occasional noises as she stirs in her sleep.*

ELLA. And this is the living room. I bought you some books. Story books. With pictures. (*She shows her the pictures.*) I wasn't sure what you'd like. Look, there's Sleeping Beauty climbing the stairs. You remember. She falls asleep for a hundred years. What a wonderful thought.

BERTHA. Sorry. I'm sorry. I'm so sorry. So sorry. Please forgive. Forgive me.

ELLA *takes the bottle from* BERTHA, *fills a glass and drinks it quickly. She looks around the room, searching for something to talk about.*

ELLA. There are hats and scarves in the cupboard . . . if you like dressing up. You can pretend to be someone else. Anyone you like. That's what grown ups do and you know it works awfully well, most of the time. The only trouble is no one knows who you really are. But then that doesn't seem to bother most people. Actually I think they rather like it that way. You're not so likely to make to make an utter fool of yourself or upset anyone or punch someone in the face or say anything you really mean.

JEAN. She tells me she wants to go to the toilet. She locks herself in and won't come out until my husband breaks the door down. Fortunately they get on rather well. He's very good with children.

BERTHA. When I first come I think it will be for a day. Two days. A week. Nights and days. Days and nights. Hundreds of them slipping through my fingers. (BERTHA *repeats under* ELLA.)

ELLA (*writing*). When I first come I think it will be for a day. Two days. A week. Nights and days. Days and nights. Hundreds of them slipping through . . .

ELLA*'s* HUSBAND *enters with her* DAUGHTER. *He is dripping wet.* ELLA *is in bed with* BERTHA *writing, surrounded by a sea of pieces of paper.*

BERTHA *continues to speak beneath the dialogue.*

HUSBAND (*to* DAUGHTER). Take off your wet shoes. (*To* ELLA.) Hello.

ELLA. I thought . . . I thought you said you were going out for the day. You took a picnic.

HUSBAND. It's raining.

ELLA. I'm writing.

HUSBAND. So I see.

ELLA. There must be somewhere dry you could . . . Madame Tussaud's.

HUSBAND. We've been.

ELLA. The circus.

HUSBAND. Been.

ELLA. National Gallery.

HUSBAND. She's eight. You haven't said 'hello'.

ELLA. I'm. I'm busy. I . . .

BERTHA. I dream of escaping. But in my dream I know. The passages will never lead anywhere. The doors will always be shut. I know because I've been there before.

HUSBAND (*to* DAUGHTER). Come on. Let's take off your wet clothes.

ELLA (*suddenly*). No. You can't. I can't have you here. There must be somewhere you can go. I mean . . .

BERTHA. I can hear sounds from a long way off. Somewhere far away in the house. I can hear laughter and I know that they talking about me.

ELLA. There must be something you could do.

BERTHA. I try to listen but they speak quietly so that I can't hear them. Then they laugh. It gets louder and louder.

ELLA (*to her* HUSBAND). All morning the people upstairs have been hammering. Hammering and talking. Then downstairs starts playing music. The same song round and round until I'm ready to go down and smash the record.

ELLA *bangs on the floor. Shut up.*

BERTHA *shouts through the floor boards.*

BERTHA. Shut the . . . Shut up. Shut it. Shut your . . . Shut the . . .

ELLA *gets hold of her and wrestles with her stifling her mouth with her hand. They struggle as* ELLA *forces* BERTHA *to the ground.*

ELLA. Shut up. Shut up. Shut up. Shut up.

The court.

JEAN. Jean Rhys was accused of attacking Mr Jones in his own home causing actual bodily harm by biting his upper arm in three places.

ELLA. Not guilty.

JEAN. When the officer arrived at the scene of the crime she told him that she had attacked Mr Jones and would do it again if he continued to play his music when she was trying to write. Mr Jones expressed surprise at this statement claiming that the accused had kept the whole house awake on several previous occasions when she and her husband had argued. One of these arguments resulted in a typewriter being thrown from a first-floor window.

ELLA. Not Guilty.

JEAN. When Mr Jones took it upon himself to complain the accused used language so vulgar he refused to repeat it to the police officer.

BERTHA *prises* ELLA*'s hands away from her mouth and screams obscenities.*

BERTHA. Eesalop. You filthy lie. You talking out your. Vieux salop. Ti lange mamau. You touch me I kill you.

ELLA *tries to cover her mouth.*

ELLA. Where are we going?

JEAN. To Holloway prison. To a cell ten feet long and four feet wide. There is nothing but a bed. There is a window too high to see out of. They take away your hair pins and shoe laces and cut your nails.

BERTHA. Cut your nails. Can't cut off your fingers. Take your hair pins. Can't take out your teeth. Take my shoe laces. Leave me my feet to run.

ELLA. I ask for books from the library. I am not allowed to go and choose. I must take what I am given. Anything to shut her out. To shut her up.

BERTHA. Them sneering. Them laughing at me. Think I don't understand. Think I is stupid. Think I/ don't know nothing . . .

ELLA. I can't stand it.

BERTHA. Say I is never any good. Say I is something broken. Smashed up. Stopped ticking. (BERTHA *continues to repeat under the dialogue.*)

ELLA. They arrive the next day. A shabby pile.

She picks up the books reading aloud the titles. A motley collection.

The English Cottage Garden, Cobbett's Advice to Young Men, The Cloister and the Hearth, Jane Eyre.

BERTHA. Them is the ones who is stupid. Them gonna find out. Them don't know nothing. Laughing. Always laughing. Saying them bad things. (*Repeats under dialogue.*)

ELLA (*reading from* Jane Eyre). She would get drunk and then erupt in outbreaks of violent and unreasonable temper. She had an appetite for every kind of excess, and yes . . . for other men. I lived with that woman for four years at the end of which the doctors declared her mad. She was shut up in her bedroom and tended by a nurse. You could hear her curses night and day. No harlot ever had a fouler vocabulary than she.

BERTHA *shouts obscenities. She continues muttering under the next speech.*

ELLA *flicks through the pages.*

To England then I conveyed her. A fearful voyage with such a monster in the vessel. Glad was I when I got her safely to the countryside and lodged in that third-storey room. That secret chamber of which she has for ten years made a wild beast's den.

BERTHA *shouts.*

ELLA (*to* JEAN). What can I do?

JEAN. Write it.

ELLA. What.

JEAN. Her story.

ELLA. My story.

JEAN. Right back. From the beginning. From the start. Everything.

ELLA. Why?

JEAN. Because you were there.

ELLA. But what about Charlotte Brontë . . . (*Indicating the book.*)

JEAN (*taking the book*). She had never tasted a mango or seen one rot in the midday heat. She didn't know that fabric rots. That furniture falls apart. That everything decays as quickly as it grows. That the road they built returned to forest. (*Beat.*) She had never seen the wide Sargasso Sea.

ELLA *picks up a pen and paper.*

We hear the sounds of the rain forest.

TITE *enters. She swipes* Jane Eyre *from* JEAN'*s hand.*

TITE. You want me take you somewhere you never been before? Yes or no?

There is a knocking at the door of the room. JEAN'*s* DAUGHTER *is standing outside. She is wearing her coat, still wet from rain.*

DAUGHTER. Mother . . . I'm still here.

BERTHA (*responding to* TITE). Where?

JEAN. I thought you . . .

DAUGHTER. The phone box is broken.

JEAN. Yes. It always is.

TITE (*to* BERTHA). Yes or no?

BERTHA. Give me my book back.

DAUGHTER. I walked to the pub. Apparently you have to book taxis three days in advance.

JEAN. Did you book one?

TITE. Yes or no?

DAUGHTER. Mother . . . I need to ask you something. The woman. The one from the shop. She asked me . . . She wanted to know . . . Were we . . . Are we . . .

JEAN. Yes?

DAUGHTER. Close.

Silence.

I didn't know what to say.

JEAN. What did you say?

Silence.

DAUGHTER. When I was a child and you used to come and visit me in the convent and we never knew what to talk about. You used to say 'Let's make up a story' and I'd say 'what about' and you'd say 'whatever's in your imagination' but there was nothing in my imagination except . . . except . . . you. So you'd make it all up instead. Fantastic stories that went on for hours and all the time I'd be looking at you and I had this feeling that although I never knew what to say to you . . . that I knew everything about you. That underneath the make up and the dressing up and the stories I knew everything. I knew about the other woman that you didn't want me to meet and I knew that was why I couldn't come to live with you.

BERTHA (*standing*). Yes.

TITE *runs.* BERTHA *follows.*

DAUGHTER. Mother. Did you hear me?

JEAN. Yes.

JEAN *watches* TITE *and* BERTHA *as they run using the furniture like a landscape. They are running through the forest to the river. We hear the sound of the water and the rainforest.*

JEAN *pulls the latch across on the door. The door opens. Her* DAUGHTER *enters the room.*

JEAN *goes to sit beside* ELLA. *She takes the paper and pen from her hand. She watches* TITE *and* BERTHA *and begins to write.* ELLA *stands and exits through the open wardrobe.*

JEAN's DAUGHTER *looks around the room. The room is in chaos with several weeks hard drinking in evidence. As* JEAN *starts to write her* DAUGHTER *begins to clear up. She stops to read a piece of manuscript she has picked up from the floor.*

TITE. I dare you. I dare you to swim to the bottom like you say you can. Right down to the bottom. Pick up a stone and bring it back.

ELLA. I can.

TITE. I ain't never seen you.

ELLA. So.

TITE. Prove it.

ELLA. Don't have to prove anything.

TITE. You scared.

ELLA. I'm not.

TITE. Bet you can't. Bet you my pen knife. Bet you my knife and this stick and my new dress and a penny and . . .

JEAN *writes as* BERTHA *and* TITE *make their way to the river's edge disappearing behind the wardrobe.*

JEAN *and* DAUGHTER *are alone on stage.* JEAN *writes as her* DAUGHTER *reads.*